D0438677

Object-Oriented Analysis

Selected titles from the YOURDON PRESS COMPUTING SERIES
Ed Yourdon, *Advisor*

Object-Oriented Analysis
Second Edition

Peter Coad and Edward Yourdon

YOURDON PRESS
PRENTICE HALL BUILDING
ENGLEWOOD CLIFFS, NJ 07632

Editorial/production supervision: BARBARA MARTTINE
Manufacturing buyer: KELLY BEHR/SUSAN BRUNKE
Photos by: DON ROGERS PHOTOGRAPHY–Austin, Texas USA
All OOA drawings in this text were developed using Object International's OOATool™.

© 1991, 1990 by Object International, Inc.

Published by Prentice-Hall, Inc.
A Division of Simon & Schuster
Englewood Cliffs, New Jersey 07632

The publisher offers discounts on this book when ordered
in bulk quantities. For more information, write:
    Special Sales/College Marketing
    College Technical and Reference Division
    Prentice Hall
    Englewood Cliffs, New Jersey 07632

OOATool™, OOAdvisor™, and The Coad Letter™ are trademarks of Object International, Inc.
Smalltalk/V® is a registered trademark of Digitalk, Inc.
ClassicAda™ is a trademark of Software Productivity Solutions.
Apple® and Macintosh® are registered trademarks of Apple Computer, Inc.
IBM® is a registered trademark of International Business Machines.
Post-it™ is a trademark of 3M.
ObjectPlus™ is a trademark of Easyspec, Inc.
Adagen™ is a trademark of Mark V Systems, Ltd.

All rights reserved. No part of this book may be
reproduced, in any form or by any means,
without permission in writing from the publisher.

Printed in the United States of America

10 9 8 7 6 5 4

ISBN   0-13-629981-4

Prentice-Hall International (UK) Limited, *London*
Prentice-Hall of Australia Pty. Limited, *Sydney*
Prentice-Hall Canada Inc., *Toronto*
Prentice-Hall Hispanoamericana, S.A., *Mexico*
Prentice-Hall of India Private Limited, *New Delhi*
Prentice-Hall of Japan, Inc., *Tokyo*
Simon & Schuster Asia Pte. Ltd., *Singapore*
Editora Prentice-Hall do Brasil, Ltda., *Rio de Janeiro*

Dedication

To Judy, my best friend—this achievement is ours.
With love,
PC

To the editors, proofreaders, artists, printers, and myriad others
behind the scenes without whose quiet, patient efforts
a book like this would never see the light of day.
EY

Contents

Preface to the Second Edition

OOA—Object-Oriented Analysis—is a relatively young method. We are committed to the continued development of OOA—in practice and in writing.

This second edition goes well beyond the first edition, incorporating these major advances:

Terminology and Notation. The second edition defines and applies the terms "class" and "object" in light of their meanings established over the centuries (rather than in light of their meanings established by analysts over a few decades). The OOA notation reflects the distinction between class and object, too.

Finding Class-&-Objects. Chapter 3 expands and refines the strategy of "where to look, what to look for, and what to consider or challenge." The strategy places extra emphasis on examining the problem domain and establishing the system's responsibilities in that context.

Identifying Structures. Chapter 4 examines the concept of Structure. Structure expresses the complexity of a problem domain, pertinent to a system's responsibilities. "Structure" is used as an overall term, describing both Generalization-Specialization (Gen-Spec) Structure and Whole-Part Structure. Chapter 4 includes Gen-Spec Structure hierarchies and lattices (i.e., single and multiple inheritance). It also adds several variations of Whole-Part Structures—assembly-parts, container-contents, and collection-members.

Defining Attributes. Chapter 6 adds strategy steps, stronger Attribute constraints, and an overall emphasis on what an Object is responsible for knowing over time (its state).

Defining Services. Chapter 7 adds both notation and strategy steps, emphasizing what an Object is responsible for doing (its behavior). The chapter adds Object State Diagrams and Service Charts; in practice, the content of our specifications has improved significantly with these additions.

OOA & CASE. We used a CASE tool for all examples in the second edition. The second edition includes a business reply card, offering a small project edition of OOA*Tool*™ at nominal cost. With this, we establish a trend for other authors to follow: here's a method *and* an inexpensive tool—to accelerate the method into practice.

Moving to OOD. Chapter 9 presents an overview of our investigative research into Object-Oriented Design, to be further expanded in our upcoming book on this topic.

Getting Started with OOA. This chapter addresses key issues related to introducing OOA into an organization.

We genuinely thank Prentice Hall for the opportunity to incorporate these advances into this second edition.

Peter Coad
Object International, Inc.
Austin, Texas
USA

Edward Yourdon
New York City, New York
USA

Acknowledgments

From Peter Coad:
First, special thanks (and love) to two extraordinary teachers—ones who have instilled a passion for excellent teaching within me—the Drs. Mr. and Mrs. Peter Coad Sr. (Hi, Mom and Dad!).

Next, a warm thank you to my clients and seminar delegates in Australia, Canada, Great Britain, Germany, France, Israel, Italy, Sweden, and the United States. So much of what OOA is today is a direct result of your thoughtful considerations and suggestions. I remain most grateful to you.

I'm very thankful for those who have allowed me to work with them on OOA, including Bob Holibaugh (Software Engineering Institute), Charles Pitcher and Al Woolfrey (Canadian Imperial Bank of Commerce), Trevor Moore (NSW State Rail, Australia), Christer Hoberg and Mats Weidmar (Enea Data, Sweden), Margaret Jenny (Mitre), Tom Turba and Linda Huebscher (Unisys), Aub Chapman (Westpac Banking Corporation, Australia), Fred Hills (Software Productivity Consortium), Dave Blue and Mike King (CTA), and Jay Crawford (Naval Weapons Center).

And thank you to those who encouraged and helped me through the years, including: Mark Mitchell, Larry Young, Tom Huchel (Technology Training Corp.); Tammy Rimmer (JPL); Tom Jensen, Karen Reynolds (Hughes Aircraft Company); Lin Conger (Marvelin Corp.); Howard Metcalfe, Dick Brewer, Bruce Eckoff, Penny Bevier (Telos Corp.); Bob Braden, Sandy Barling (Texas Dept. of Motor Vehicles); Ralph Kirkley (Ralph Kirkley Associates); and Vicki Munro (Naval Weapons Center).

From Ed Yourdon:
Thanks to a number of people who have urged me during the past several years to focus more on an object-oriented view of the world: Dave Bulman, Mike Silves, Larry Proctor, Steve and Greta Blash, and the late Matt Flavin.

From both of us:
Thanks also to a group of authors whose work in the field over the past decade has helped lay a foundation for our work in this book:

Grady Booch, Brad Cox, Bertrand Meyer, Adele Goldberg, Michael Jackson, Chris Gane, Ed Berard, and Ken Orr.

Thanks to the official reviewers of the first edition, for their patient readings and valuable insights: Sam Adams (Knowledge Systems Corporation), Alan Davis (George Mason University), Tom Jensen (Hughes Aircraft Company), Charles McKay (University of Houston, Clear Lake), Michael Rissman (Software Engineering Institute), and Ed Seidewitz (Goddard Space Flight Center).

Thanks to Toni for her cheerful editing work. And thanks to the Prentice Hall staff that worked so diligently with us in producing this book, including Bernard Goodwin, Paul Becker, Barbara Marttine, and Noreen Regina.

From both of us, in preparing the second edition:
We are very grateful to five special reviewers:
Sam Adams (Knowledge Systems Corporation)
Alan Davis (George Mason University)
Tom Jensen (Hughes Aircraft Company)
Jeff McKenna (McKenna Consulting Group)
Ragan Wilkinson (Object International, Inc.)
The second edition is far better as a result of their kind help and valuable advice.

Thanks to our colleagues at Knowledge Systems Corporation— Sam Adams, Ken Auer, Steve Burbeck, Reed Phillips, and S. Sridhar (plus Larry Marran from HP). And thanks to Hermann Schindler (Advanced Micro Devices).

Thank you to the Prentice Hall staff that worked together with us on this second edition, including Bernard Goodwin, Paul Becker, Barbara Marttine, and Noreen Regina. Plus, thanks to Karen Comstock and her colleagues at Morgan-Cain & Associates (Tucson, Arizona USA).

0

Introduction

OOA—Object-Oriented Analysis—is based upon concepts that we first learned in kindergarten: objects and attributes, wholes and parts, classes and members. Why it has taken us so long to apply these concepts to the analysis and specification of information systems is anyone's guess—perhaps we've been too busy "following the flow" during the heyday of structured analysis to consider the alternatives.

As the *Encyclopaedia Britannica* points out:

> In apprehending the real world, men [people] constantly employ three methods of organization, which pervade all of their thinking:
>
> (1) the differentiation of experience into particular objects and their attributes—e.g., when they distinguish between a tree and its size or spatial relations to other objects,
>
> (2) the distinction between whole objects and their component parts—e.g., when they contrast a tree with its component branches, and
>
> (3) the formation of and the distinction between different classes of objects—e.g., when they form the class of all trees and the class of all stones and distinguish between them.
>
> [Britannica, "Classification Theory," 1986]

The notation and approach of OOA builds upon these three constantly employed methods of organization.

Several years ago, one of the authors consulted, during a two-and-a-half year period, on the practical application of real-time structured analysis on a major air traffic control project. His observations were interesting and yet disturbing. One team of analysts (the "DFD Team") started their projects using data flow diagrams to develop an overall functional decomposition, as a framework for further specification. Meanwhile, a second team of analysts (the "Data Base Team") started by focusing on the information the system needed to do its job and then building an information model (also known as an Entity-Relationship Diagram or a Semantic Data Model).

Over time, the DFD Team continued to struggle with basic problem domain understanding (e.g., the details of what happens when one controller hands off responsibility for an aircraft to another controller). In contrast, the Data Base Team gained a strong, in-depth understanding of air traffic control. Yet the results of the two teams did not mesh together; worse, they contradicted each other. In principle, these two models should somehow come together. Yet under the pressures of schedule and budget, the results were pushed into preliminary design, with the hope of resolving the discrepancies at that time. Sadly, the Data Base Team was perceived as irksome, even somewhat as troublemakers; people (and their careers) paid the price for this major rift and its untidy resolution.

A few years later, the same author saw this same pattern develop on projects at a federal government agency and a state government agency. The DFD Team marched on, ahead in time and political power. The Data Base Team gained tremendous insight, vital to analysis but all too often ignored. And again, the Data Base Team and its leader were perceived as troublemakers.

Repeatedly, *in practice,* separate notations and strategies for different process and data models have kept the two forever apart. Because of this chasm, we began the research and development of a method—notations and strategies—that would help analysts gain the much-needed problem domain understanding first, and then add the behavior (processing) requirements within the framework of that solid understanding. We put the method to work in practice, refining and building the approach into a systematic method. Over the past few years, both authors have presented the method to top professionals in Austria, Australia, Brazil, Canada, Denmark, Great Britain, Germany, France, Hong Kong, India, Israel, Italy, Japan, the Netherlands, Singapore, South Africa, Spain, Sweden, and the United States, receiving valuable feedback and insight from the delegates. In applying OOA on actual projects, both clients and seminar participants significantly contributed to the development of this method.

0.1 ORGANIZATION

This book presents OOA in ten chapters.

Chapters 1 and 2 lay the foundation. "Improving Analysis" examines the challenge of systems analysis, and then reviews some principles for managing complexity. It then summarizes four popular analysis methods: Functional Decomposition, Data Flow, Information Modeling, and Object-Oriented. Chapter 2, "Experiencing An Object Perspective," explores a fully object-oriented programming language and environment to illustrate some key points for usc in OOA.

Chapters 3 through 7 cover the OOA method in five major activities: Finding Class-&-Objects, Identifying Structures, Identifying Subjects, Defining Attributes, and Defining Services. Each chapter is organized into What, Why, How, and Key Points (a concise summary).

Chapter 8, "Selecting CASE for OOA," describes Computer-Aided Software Engineering (CASE) support for OOA, showing what is needed and what is currently available.

Chapter 9 moves into Object-Oriented Design (OOD), describing design considerations and what happens to the OOA model as OOD proceeds.

Finally, Chapter 10 addresses key issues related to introducing OOA into an organization.

Appendix A presents a concise summary of OOA notations and strategies. It also includes an OOA model of OOA itself.

Appendix B illustrates how to apply OOA when working with the U.S. Defense Department's DOD-STD-2167A, *Defense System Software Development.*

0.2 WHY DO WE NEED OOA?

The key motivations and benefits for OOA are presented here, to help two kinds of readers. For the manager, this section highlights why he might encourage his subordinates to use OOA. For the technical staff member, this section presents rationale that he may use to convince a manager to let him use OOA.

The motivations and benefits are as follows:

1. *Tackle more challenging problem domains.* OOA brings extra emphasis to the understanding of problem domains.

2. *Improve analyst and problem domain expert interaction.* OOA organizes analysis and specification using the methods of organization which pervade people's thinking.

3. *Increase the internal consistency of analysis results.* OOA reduces the bandwidth between different analysis activities, by treating Attributes and Services as an intrinsic whole.

4. *Explicitly represent commonality.* OOA uses inheritance to identify and capitalize on commonality of Attributes and Services.

5. *Build specifications resilient to change.* OOA packages volatility within problem-domain constructs, providing stability over changing requirements and similar systems.

6. *Reuse analysis results,* accommodating both families of systems and practical tradeoffs within a system. OOA organizes results based upon problem domain constructs, for present reuse and for future reuse.

7. *Provide a consistent underlying representation* for analysis (what is to be built) and design (how it is to be built this time). OOA establishes a continuum of representation, for systematically expanding analysis results into a specific design.

0.3 AUDIENCE

We have aimed this book at the practicing systems analyst, the person who has to tackle real-world systems development projects every day. We assume a fundamental understanding of computer technology and systems analysis concepts, and we expect that many of our readers will have had some experience with such analysis tools as data flow diagrams and entity relationship diagrams. Managers, testers, standards bearers, and clients can read the book and expect to profit from the overall approach to improving systems analysis.

For managers, we suggest that you begin with the key issues related to introducing OOA into an organization (Chapter 10). Then proceed to the chapters on improving analysis (Chapter 1) and on CASE (Chapter 8). Finally, for added technical detail, read the other chapters.

0.4 FOCUS AND HISTORY

Though it will become abundantly clear in the following chapters, we should stress here that our concern in this book is with object-oriented *analysis,* not Object-Oriented Programming (OOP) or Object-Oriented Design (OOD). Systems analysts first must understand the problem domain at hand; it makes little sense to run off and start writing air traffic control functional requirements—let alone thinking about design architectures or writing code—without first studying, expressing, and validating our understanding of what air traffic control is really all about. Objects as abstractions of the real world provide a focus on significant aspects of the problem domain and the system's responsibilities; ultimately this knowledge results in a tangible, reviewable, and manageable collection of model layers (Subject, Class-&-Object, Structure, Attribute, and Service) produced during the five major activities of OOA.

We could argue that this perspective has *always* been important, even if it has not been a terribly popular one. If this is the case, then why this book on OOA? Why has the "object paradigm" finally come of age? Why now?

Object-oriented *programming* was first discussed in the late 1960s by those working with the SIMULA language. By the 1970s, it was an important part of the Smalltalk language developed at Xerox PARC. Meanwhile, the rest of the world bumbled along with languages like COBOL and FORTRAN, and used functional decomposition methods (which we will discuss in more detail in Chapter 1) to address problems of design and implementation. Little, if any, discussion focused on object-oriented *design,* and virtually none on object-oriented *analysis.*

Four changes have occurred over the past decade, and are now key factors as we enter the 1990s:

- The underlying concepts of an object-oriented approach have had a decade to mature, and attention has gradually shifted from issues of coding, to issues of design, to issues of analysis. The proponents of functional decomposition spent a decade progressing from structured programming to structured design to structured analysis; we should not be surprised to see the same progression in the object-oriented world.

- The underlying technology for building systems has become much more powerful. Unfortunately, our way of thinking about systems analysis is influenced by our preconceived ideas of how we would design a system to meet its requirements; our ideas about design are influenced by our preconceived ideas about how we would write code; and our ideas about coding are strongly influenced by the programming languages we have available. It was difficult to think about structured programming (and thus difficult to think about structured design and analysis) when the languages of choice were assembler, Autocoder and FORTRAN; things became easier with Pascal, PL/1, ALGOL, FORTRAN-77, Structured BASIC, and newer versions of COBOL. Similarly, it was difficult to think about coding in an object-oriented fashion when the language of choice was COBOL, FORTRAN, or plain-vanilla C; it has become easier with C++, Objective-C, Smalltalk, and Ada.

- The systems we build today are different than they were ten or twenty years ago. In every respect, they are larger and more complex; they are also more volatile and subject to constant change. We will argue in subsequent chapters that an object-oriented approach to analysis (and design) is likely to lead to a more stable system. Also, we find that today's on-line, interactive systems devote much more attention to the *user interface* than the text-oriented batch processing systems of the 1960s and 1970s. Some observers, such as Bill Joy of Sun Microsystems, argue that as much as 75 percent of the code in a modern system may be concerned with the user interface—e.g., manipulating windows, pull-down menus, icons, mouse movements, etc.; this is particularly evident with the graphical user interface available on Apple Macintosh, IBM OS/2 Presentation Manager, and Microsoft Windows. Our experience has been that an object-oriented approach to such systems—from analysis through design and into coding—is a more natural way of dealing with such user-oriented systems.

- Many organizations find that the systems they build today are more "data-oriented" than the systems they built in the 1970s and 1980s. Functional complexity is less of a concern than it was before; modeling the data has become a higher priority.

0.5 METHOD AND TOOL

With this book, we'd like to set a trend: present a method *and* a low cost drawing and checking tool to try it out. The tool presented in this book is OOA*Tool*™.

To provide you with a *small project version* of OOA*Tool*™ at nominal cost, a business reply card is included in this book (if the card is gone, please write for details). Send the card to Peter Coad at Object International, Inc., 3202 W. Anderson Lane, Suite 208–724, Austin, Texas 78757–1022, USA.

All OOA examples in this book were developed using OOA*Tool*™.

0.6 FUTURE ADVANCES IN OOA

OOA is a relatively young method; it will continue to evolve in practice. So we implore you, the reader, not to come up to us at computer conferences and say that you are developing systems "compliant with the Coad/Yourdon OOA standard." Rather, use this book as a starting point for applying OOA—tailoring and expanding the method to suit your specific organization or project needs.

To provide you with updates on OOA, a business reply card offering free special reports, *The Coad Letter™: New Advances in Object-Oriented Analysis and Design*, is included in this book (if the card is gone, please write for details). Send the card to Peter Coad at Object International, Inc., 3202 W. Anderson Lane, Suite 208–724, Austin, Texas 78757–1022, USA.

In addition, ongoing developments in OOA and OOD are discussed in Ed Yourdon's monthly software journal, *American Programmer*. For a complimentary sample issue, contact Ed Yourdon at American Programmer, Inc., Dept. 13, 161 West 86th Street, New York, NY 10024–3411.

We expect to further develop OOA over time. Some of the issues under consideration include the following:

1. Putting together dozens of OOA models from other practitioners, and describing the patterns observed and lessons learned across a wide variety of problem domains.
2. Developing OOD as a multi-layer, multi-component model.
3. Developing cost estimation techniques specifically for Object-Oriented Development.
4. Adding guidelines for risk identification, risk analysis, and risk management specifically for Object-Oriented Development.

1

Improving Analysis

In this chapter, we examine the analysis challenge, principles for managing complexity, and analysis methods, including an overview of OOA.

1.1 THE ANALYSIS CHALLENGE

Systems analysis exhilarates and exasperates those who fall prey to its siren song. What is so difficult about analysis? What is the challenge? We feel that four major difficulties plague systems analysts on all types of projects: problem domain understanding, person-to-person communication, continual change, and reuse.

1.1.1 The Problem Domain and the System's Responsibilities

One of the biggest problems faced by analysts is studying the problem domain and making discoveries about it.

In fact, analysts need to investigate the problem domain and the system's responsibilities within that problem domain. The terms "problem domain" and "system's responsibilities" help make a needed distinction for effective analysis.

> Problem. [to throw forward, to drive forward (Greek)] A question proposed for solution or consideration
>
> Domain. [right of ownership, dominion (Greek)] The sphere or field of activity or influence; as the *domain* of art or politics
>
> [Webster's, 1977]

And so—

> Problem Domain. A field of endeavor under consideration.

Examples of problem domains include air space management, avionics, finance, and law.

One aspect of OOA is gaining an understanding of the problem domain. And then the analyst focuses in on those matters pertinent to his work, namely, describing the responsibilities of the system under consideration.

> System. [to place together (Greek)] A set or arrangement of things so related or connected as to form a unity or organic whole; as, a solar *system*, irrigation *system*, supply *system*.
>
> Responsibility. [requiring an answer (Greek)] The condition, quality, fact, or instance of being responsible, answerable, accountable, or liable, as for a person, trust, office, or debt.
>
> [Webster's, 1977]

And so—

> System's Responsibilities. An arrangement of things accountable for, related together as a whole.

OOA is the challenge of understanding the problem domain, and then the system's responsibilities in that light. As consultants, the authors have usually experienced this problem in an extreme form: we were dropped into a project for a week, a month, or occasionally as long as a year. In most cases, we couldn't pretend at all to be subject matter experts in the client's business or application. We needed to grasp, to understand in depth, the problem domain—and we needed to do it as quickly as possible. Of course, the situation is less extreme for many systems analysts—but even if you happen to be a subject matter expert as well as an analyst, you still need tools to effectively communicate your expertise to others on your team. For example, if you have been working with radar systems for the past 20 years, you probably have intimate knowledge of the problem domain; if the time has come to specify the requirements for yet another radar system, your primary problem may be that of communicating with other radar experts as well as project members who can't distinguish a radar from a grapefruit.

Analysts must consider the problem domain in which they work. For example, consider the problem of air traffic control. The analyst needs to immerse himself in that problem domain, immerse himself so deeply that he begins to discover nuances that even those who live with air traffic control every day have not yet fully considered. As another example, consider a business system that maintains information about motor vehicle registrations and titles; an analyst working on such a system would need to study and assimilate all sorts of details—and many exceptions to the rules, resulting from special interest group demands and the statutes that follow.

This discussion has described a major part of what it is to be an effective analyst. It's much more than just writing some observable, measurable functional requirements. Yes, an analyst needs to specify requirements, concisely packaged so that fellow human beings can read and understand what the analyst believes those requirements are. But understanding the problem domain is really the crux of systems analysis.

If an analyst simply assumes that he has subject matter knowledge, he is likely to indulge in thinking that will lead to fuzzy requirements. One of the authors was recently involved in a large air traffic control project, in which requirements analysts were still grappling with basic air traffic control concepts even after two years of specifying software requirements. This situation should not have occurred. Analysts need to understand and model the problem domain, *especially* for large, complex systems; with such understanding, the textual specification of measurable requirements can be done in a fairly straightforward fashion.[1]

1.1.2 Communication

The analysis challenge also requires effective communication. An analyst needs to communicate throughout the analysis effort. He must communicate just to extract information about the problem domain and requirements from the client. He thinks about all of this communication and refines it himself. He interacts with his peers. Ultimately, he needs to echo his problem domain understanding and subsequent requirements back to the client, to validate his understanding of the requirements. He may also need help in steering his client away from requirements that cannot be met within budget and schedule constraints.

A funny irony exists in the term "software engineering": though the words conjure up images of formulas, algorithms, and "hard" scientific approaches, software engineering is actually a very people-oriented business. Recently, one of the authors spoke at a conference in Chicago and was asked if OOA (and/or other software methods) was the key to successful software development. The response? Yes, having a consistent technical approach is very valuable. Yet software methods are effective only to the extent that they help people to

[1] Regardless of the method or modeling approach, it is unlikely that an analyst will fully understand the problem domain and the system's responsibilities at the beginning of a project. Analysis is a process of continual learning about the nuances of a problem domain and the system's responsibilities.

communicate with one another. If the application of a software engineering "method" produces a monument of paper, then something is wrong—in the method, in the application of the method, or perhaps both. If we lose sight of people and begin producing charts, diagrams, and piles of paper as ends unto themselves, we fail to effectively communicate. Software engineering is a people business. People make the problems; people solve the problems. And we can solve our systems development problems only by interacting with each other.

At this same computer conference, the beleaguered author then did a "bad" thing. He asked how many educators in the audience required some interpersonal communications training as part of their software engineering program. *No hands were raised.* Yet effective communication—with management, peers, reviewers, standards bearers, and clients—is vital to successful systems analysis.

Viable software methods must facilitate communication. Successful software methods build upon human methods of organization, rather than upon a contrived notation that works well for computation (e.g., "follow the flow") but not for humans.

1.1.3 Continual Change

The requirements for a system will always be in a state of flux. Management or clients may impose an artificial freezing of requirements at a particular point in time. But the *true* requirements, the needed system, will continue to evolve. Many forces affect this ever-changing requirements set: clients, competition, regulators, approvers, and technologists. As Gerhard Fischer points out [Fischer, 1989], "We have to accept changing requirements as a fact of life, and not condemn them as a product of sloppy thinking."

An analyst endeavors to organize his notations and strategies so that his work is resilient to change. He seeks requirements packaging that will remain stable over time. The explicit capture of commonality is a great help here, for both data and processing. And as he finds computer implementation issues and other design considerations, he tucks them into a file folder, deferring added complexity until the requirements are put forth.

1.1.4 Reuse

Our colleague Tony Wasserman encouraged us to investigate reusable analysis results. And we've benefited greatly from Will

Tracz [Tracz, 1988a] during these investigations.

> Reuse. To put or to bring into action or service *again*; to employ for or apply to a given purpose *again*.
>
> [From "re-" and "use," Webster's, 1977]

In analysis, reuse is the act of incorporating previous analysis results into the current one. Yet very little analysis reuse has happened in the past. For example, one government contractor has built systems within the same basic problem domain over a 25 year period. The problem domain has changed very little in that much time; yet such stability over time has not been applied as a framework for communicating or reusing analysis results from one project to the next.

More effective analysis requires the use of problem domain constructs, both for present reuse and for future reuse.

Reusable analysis results carry the greatest potential for improving system development—people delivering specific capabilities within schedule and budget.

1.2 PRINCIPLES FOR MANAGING COMPLEXITY

This section sets forth these major principles for managing complexity of a problem domain and the system's responsibilities within it:

- Abstraction
  Procedural
  Data
- Encapsulation
- Inheritance
- Association
- Communication with messages
- Pervading methods of organization
  Objects and attributes
  Whole and parts
  Classes and members, and distinguishing
  between them
- Scale
- Categories of behavior
  Immediate causation
  Change over time
  Similarity of functions

Various analysis methods incorporate some or all of these principles. Here, the principles are examined. Later in the chapter, various analysis methods are examined in light of which principles they incorporate.

1.2.1 Abstraction

The first principle is abstraction:

Abstraction. The principle of ignoring those aspects of a subject that are not relevant to the current purpose in order to concentrate more fully on those that are. [Oxford, 1986]

This term means that even though an analyst knows about many things, he chooses certain things over others.

Both authors have young children whose rooms are filled with a variety of toys, many of which are small-scale replicas of airplanes, cars, and exotic warriors. It's interesting to see how even little children deal with the concept of abstraction: a little toy hook-and-ladder fire truck, for example, could have been built with a hundred-pound hose hanging off its side. But the abstraction would be out of proportion, and rendered useless for its intended user. Yet we know, and even the child knows, that the hose is there; we need its complexity in the real system; but it would be inappropriate for the abstraction our children play with on their bedroom floors.

Most of what we deal with in the real world—people, places, things, and concepts—is intrinsically complex, far more complex than we can cope with in one fell swoop. When we use abstraction, we admit that what we are considering is complex; rather than try to comprehend the entire thing, we select only part of it. We know it contains additional details; we simply choose not to use them at this time. This technique is an important way to manage complexity.

Procedural abstraction is one form of abstraction used extensively by requirements analysts, as well as designers and programmers. It's often characterized as "function/sub-function" abstraction. You may be familiar with diagramming methods such as structure charts, with the big box at the top—representing the entire system or "thing" being considered—and the subordinate steps or sub-functions shown as smaller boxes below the top-level box.

Procedural Abstraction. The principle that any operation that achieves a well-defined effect can be treated by its users as a single entity, despite the fact that the operation may actually be achieved by some sequence of lower-level operations. [Oxford, 1986]

Breaking processing (e.g., aircraft tracking) down into sub-steps is one basic method of handling complexity. But, as we will discuss in more detail below, using such a breakdown for organizing an entire analysis and specification is somewhat arbitrary and highly volatile. (Procedural abstraction is not the primary form of abstraction for OOA; however, it does come into play in OOA within the limited context of specifying and describing Services.)

Another, more powerful abstraction mechanism is data abstraction. This principle can be a basis for organization of thinking and of specification of a system's responsibilities.

Data Abstraction. The principle of defining a data type in terms of the operations that apply to objects of the type, with the constraint that the values of such objects can be modified and observed only by the use of the operations. [Oxford, 1986]

In applying data abstraction, an analyst defines Attributes. And he defines Services that exclusively manipulate those Attributes. The only way to get to the Attributes is via a Service.[2] Attributes and their Services may be treated as an intrinsic whole.

1.2.2 Encapsulation

Another principle for managing complexity is encapsulation:

Encapsulation (Information Hiding). A principle, used when developing an overall program structure, that each component of a program should encapsulate or hide a single design decision.... The interface to each module is defined in such a way as to reveal as little as possible about its inner workings. [Oxford, 1986]

This definition reflects the design work of David Parnas in the early 1970s [Parnas, 1972].

The power and attractiveness of encapsulation is that it helps minimize rework when developing a new system. If an analyst encapsulates the parts of the analysis effort that are most volatile, then the (inevitable) changing of requirements becomes less of a threat to the overall effort. Localizing volatility is essential: whether we like it or not, we as analysts live in an environment of continual

---

[2] For those familiar with other forms of systems analysis, the term "Service" is equivalent to the terms "function" or "process."

change. Encapsulation keeps related content together; it minimizes traffic between different parts of the work; and it separates certain specified requirements from other parts of the specification which may use those requirements.

1.2.3 Inheritance

Inheritance is another underlying principle of OOA:

Inheritance. A mechanism for expressing similarity among Classes, simplifying definition of Classes similar to one(s) previously defined. It portrays generalization and specialization, making common Attributes and Services explicit within a Class hierarchy or lattice.

This principle forms the basis for a significant technique of explicit expression of commonality. Inheritance allows an analyst to specify common Attributes and Services *once*, as well as specialize and extend those Attributes and Services into specific cases.

Thus, one might recognize a Vehicle Class as a generalization. A TruckVehicle Class, as a specialization, inherits Attributes and Services from "Vehicle." In addition, a specialization can add Attributes; and a specialization can add Services or extend Services it inherits. Thus, a "TruckVehicle" might have added Attributes such as "NumberOfAxles" or "NumberOfWheels," and added Services such as "Calculate MaxWeightPerAxle," which might not be relevant or appropriate for "Vehicle" in general.

Inheritance may be applied to explicitly express commonality, beginning with the early activities of analysis.

1.2.4 Association

Another principle for managing complexity is association.

Association. The union or connection of ideas.
[Webster's, 1977]

People use association to tie together certain things that happen at some point in time or under similar circumstances.

1.2.5 Communication with Messages

Webster's defines a message with the following:

Message. Any communication, written or oral, sent between persons.
[Webster's, 1977]

Message interaction corresponds to the imperative mood in languages. "The imperative mood conveys commands or requests...." [Britannica, "Imperative Mood," 1986].

A principle for managing complexity—notably for interfaces—is communication with messages.

1.2.6 Pervading Methods of Organization

It would be intellectually satisfying to the authors if we could report that we studied the philosophical ideas behind methods of organization, from Socrates and Aristotle to Descartes and Kant. Then, based on the underlying methods human beings use, we could propose the basic constructs essential to an analysis method. But in truth we cannot say that, nor did we do it.

However, we did approach the problem as practitioners and investigators. We researched and applied various software subjects, in particular semantic data modeling and object-oriented programming languages. We began to ferret out some of the embellishments, looking for the key principles that could be applied to organizing and representing requirements. We looked for the concepts that gave the greatest leverage in understanding and expressing problem domain knowledge. And we boiled everything down to three key methods of organization.

Also, we investigated *Encyclopaedia Britannica*, to read a concise summary of how people organize their thinking. Here's what we found:

> In apprehending the real world, men [people] constantly employ three methods of organization, which pervade all of their thinking:
>
> (1) the differentiation of experience into particular objects and their attributes—e.g., when they distinguish between a tree and its size or spatial relations to other objects,
>
> (2) the distinction between whole objects and their component parts—e.g., when they contrast a tree with its component branches, and
>
> (3) the formation of and the distinction between different classes of objects—e.g., when they form the class of all trees and the class of all stones and distinguish between them.
>
> [Britannica, "Classification Theory," 1986]

Analysis notation and strategy can build upon these three constantly employed methods of organization.[3]

It is worth noting that there are indeed *three* pervading methods of organization—not just one. In practice, applying "objects and attributes," "whole and parts," *and* "classes, members, and distinguishing between them" provides significantly greater insight into a problem domain and a system's responsibilities than applying only "objects and attributes."

1.2.7 Scale

A principle which applies the whole-part principle to help an observer relate to something very large—without being overwhelmed—is called "scale":

> When the proportions of architectural composition are applied to a particular building, the two-termed relationship of the parts to the whole must be harmonized with a third term—the observer. This three-termed relationship is called scale.
>
> [Britannica, "Architecture, The Art of," 1986]

With scale, analysis notation and strategy can include ways to guide a reader through a larger model.

1.2.8 Categories of Behavior

Shortly after finding the "pervading methods of organization" statement, we were asked, "Yes, but what about the active side of objects—what of their behavior?" Having gained such benefit from *Encyclopaedia Britannica* before, we turned to it once again. The section on human behavior was all too bewildering; however, we found a useful set of behavior categories, just a few pages later:

> Three types of behavior classification are used most commonly:
>
> (1) on the basis of immediate causation,
>
> (2) on similarity of evolutionary history [change over time], and
>
> (3) on the similarity of function.
>
> [Britannica, "Animal Behaviour," 1986]

---

[3] In OOA, they are referred to, respectively, as Objects and Attributes, Whole-Part Structures, and Classes (applying the aspect of "distinguishing between them" with Generalization-Specialization Structures, Attributes, and Services).

A major advance in the 1980s (circa 1982) was the addition of an event-response strategy to structured analysis; this was an application of the first of these three categories of behavior.

1.2.9 Summary of Principles

So, major principles for managing complexity of a problem domain and the system's responsibilities within it include:

*   Abstraction
    Procedural
    Data
*   Encapsulation
*   Inheritance
*   Association
*   Communication with Messages
*   Pervading methods of organization
    Objects and attributes
    Whole and parts
    Classes and members, and distinguishing
    between them
*   Scale
*   Categories of behavior
    Immediate causation
    Change over time
    Similarity of functions

Various analysis methods incorporate some or all of these principles. We'll examine this further in the pages which follow.

1.3 ANALYSIS METHODS

This section surveys four major approaches to analysis. These approaches are thinking tools, used to help in the formulation of requirements.

First, what is systems analysis? DeMarco offers the following definition [DeMarco, 1978]: "Analysis is the study of a problem, prior to taking some action."

To us, analysis is the study of a problem domain, leading to a specification of externally observable behavior; a complete, consistent, and feasible statement of what is needed; a coverage of both functional and quantified operational characteristics (e.g., reliability, availability, performance).

Analysis means the process of extracting the "needs" of a system—*what* the system must do to satisfy the client, not *how* the system will be implemented. Systems analysis usually begins with a requesting document (from the client, or perhaps from the marketing division) and a series of discussions. In any case, the audience includes clients, problem domain experts, developers, and possibly other interested parties (e.g., auditors, contracting officers, etc.) who may need to understand and agree with the proposed set of requirements. The requirements document should communicate a complete, consistent, and feasible statement of what is needed in the system. It should be manageable both before and after it is produced. Requirements include functional operations and (quantified!) operational characteristics such as ease of use, reliability, availability, maintainability, and performance. Requirements also include interfaces that the software must deal with, environments the software must accommodate, and any other applicable design constraints.

A requirements document has two purposes: (1) it formalizes the needs of the client, and (2) it establishes a list of mandates.

The first three approaches to analysis presented in this section—functional decomposition, data flow, and information modeling—have been discussed and practiced in the systems development profession for a decade or more. We have personally used all three methods on large systems, sometimes with successful results and sometimes with abject failure. The strengths of these first three methods have their place in specific contexts in the fourth method discussed in this section, OOA. We feel it is important to emphasize that we are not trying to abolish the *underlying principles* behind the older, more established methods. Software methods should be utterly pragmatic, without religious fervor. An analyst needs all the help he can get. What we are attempting to do is to incorporate the best ideas of the first three methods in a more comprehensive, all-encompassing method—OOA.

Rather than endlessly argue about which method is best, we prefer to take a pragmatic view, using whatever combination of approaches helps in a given situation, no matter which methods they come from.

Each approach is defined below with an equation, for easy recognition of the method. Each approach is also examined in light of large project experience.

1.3.1 Functional Decomposition

Functional decomposition is readily recognized with its steps and sub-steps. An equation representation useful in identifying this method is:

Functional Decomposition = Functions
+ Sub-functions
+ Functional interfaces

This representation illustrates how we recognize that something has been functionally decomposed.

The underlying strategy of functional decomposition consists of selecting the processing steps and sub-steps anticipated for a new system. Analysts use previous experience from similar systems, combined at times with an examination of required outputs. The focus is on *what processing* is required for the new system. The analyst then specifies the processing and functional interfaces.

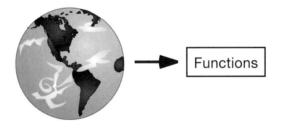

Figure 1.1: Functional Decomposition

Functional decomposition requires humans to map from problem domain (e.g., air traffic control) to functions and sub-functions. The analyst must internalize the subject matter, and then document the corresponding required functions and sub-functions that the system shall provide. The resulting specification only *indirectly* maps

[4] The indirect mapping exists even if the client provides a list of requirements. The analyst must still understand the problem domain and the system's responsibilities within it, and must verify that understanding with the client.

back to the subject matter.[4] Nothing explicitly maps the functionality back to the subject matter itself. This method makes it difficult for the analyst and the client to assess whether or not the requirements are an accurate statement of what the new system is required to do. With such an approach, problem domain understanding is neither explicitly expressed nor verified for its accuracy; subtle aspects of the problem domain are simply not uncovered.

Is functional decomposition bad? No! After all, eventually both data and data processing must be specified. In fact, OOA uses functional decomposition (gasp!), albeit in a very specific context: defining a Service—a specific behavior that an Object is responsible for exhibiting. In other words, it may be helpful to break up a large, complicated Service into smaller pieces for convenience in stating what is required. For example, an analyst will probably divide a description of a "Monitor" Service into a number of smaller pieces. He may also use a block diagram or data flow diagram fragment to help guide the reader through the requirements of this Service. But this definition is all done within a very limited context; the processing steps are not used as the primary organizational framework during analysis or specification; processing steps are too volatile over time.

Function/sub-function breakdowns are difficult to construct (because of the indirect mapping) and highly volatile (because of the continual change of functional capability which may be successfully delivered within budget and schedule constraints). For these reasons, we feel that the overall analysis approach should *not* be based on function/sub-function; a more stable analysis viewpoint and specification organization is needed.

In functional decomposition, analysts end up with system, subsystem, function, and sub-function levels. The problem lies in choosing the functions and knowing the potential volatility of system functionality. Another problem facing the analyst is choosing the functions and sub-functions in such a way that the interface bandwidth is minimized, both now and over time. Though earlier textbooks (see, for example, Yourdon and Constantine, 1979, and Page-Jones, 1988) used the concepts of *coupling* and *cohesion* to describe the composition of system components and the interfaces between those components, many system developers had a difficult time identifying sub-functions so that when a processing change came, they captured the new requirements with a minimum of change to the analysis and specification organization.

1.3.2 Data Flow Approach

Another method (and another way to map problem domain and the system's responsibilities into a technical representation) is the data flow approach, often described as "structured analysis." One can recognize a data flow approach with this equation:

Data Flow Approach = Data (& control) flows

+ Data (& control) transformations

+ Data (& control) stores

+ Terminators

+ Process Specs (mini-specs)

+ Data Dictionary

This notation is basic. Sometimes an information model (by various names, e.g., Entity-Relationship Diagrams) is used too; these models will be discussed later in this chapter.

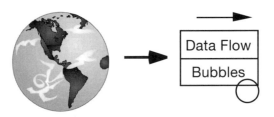

Figure 1.2: Data Flow Approach

With this method, the analyst maps from the real world into data flows and bubbles. This mapping requires the analyst (and more significantly, the client) to follow the flow of data whenever looking at the real world, and map that flow into subsequent analysis and specification. Yet "follow the flow of data" is not one of the basic methods many humans use to manage complexity when looking at a problem domain. In other words, it is not one of the basic methods of organization that pervade people's thinking. Considering an event (e.g., a transaction request) and then identifying the processing steps taken in response to that event is quite helpful, and is in fact one of the strategies in OOA for identifying Services and the steps within a Service. But this flow describes processing steps (using procedural abstraction), not the flow of data and its gradual refinement (which is a thinking approach that leads to procedural abstraction).

Two major strategies predominate in structured analysis. The "old" method (see DeMarco, 1978, and Gane and Sarson, 1977) maps the current system to data flow diagrams, removes the physical idiosyncrasies, adds new logical requirements, and then adds new physical considerations.

For the current U.S. Air Traffic Control System, or for many states' registration and title systems, the documentation of client requirements of the existing system consisted of little more than source code and patched object code from the late 1960s. Studying and modeling such systems was, in effect, studying and modeling a prior mapping of the problem domain, rather than the problem domain itself. Analysts find it difficult to recover from this misplaced focus of study.

The problems with this older strategy became apparent as team after team got ensnared as they attempted to model the current system, while time, budget, and patience wore out. Analysts just did not know when to stop (and when in doubt, kept adding to the model). As our colleague Steve McMenamin observes, many analysts fell into the "current physical tarpit," never to emerge.

The "modern" structured analysis approach first appeared in seminars as early as 1982, in books as early as 1984 (see, for example, McMenamin and Palmer, 1984), and more recently in *Modern Structured Analysis* in 1989 [Yourdon, 1989]. The strategy developed because analysts had problems picking bubbles for their data flow diagrams. So, to assist in picking the bubbles, the first step is to define events. Events are those occurrences in the outside world that a planned-response system must respond to.[5] Each event corresponds to a bubble; for a system with 150 events, draw 150 bubbles. Name each bubble by deciding what the system does in response to the event. Add appropriate input and output flows to each bubble. Place data stores between bubbles that need to communicate with data held over time. Then, group the bubbles into page-size bites. Next, draw higher-level summaries, up two or three levels, the highest of which is a "context diagram" in which the entire system is shown as a single bubble. For lower-level bubbles, apply functional decomposition to define even lower levels, as needed.

[5] The actual interaction between the user and the system is message-based. The event list documented in the "modern" approach to structured analysis is largely a documentation of the individual requests made by human users, so that the event and data flow correspondence can be expressed. Using a message-based interaction model expresses the correspondence directly.

The additional documentation needed includes specifying the data flows and bottom-level transformations with a data dictionary and process specifications, respectively. The upper level diagrams exist to provide a big picture for the reader; the process specification content expresses the detail. But much of the lower level detail must be understood for the graphical summaries to make much sense.

The challenge is in how to pick the bubbles. Event-response partitioning can help. But with too many events, the number of bubbles gets out of hand. And little help is given on making groups of higher levels to improve human understandability—the guideline "group bubbles that deal with common data stores" sounds sensible, but often breaks down in practice. Far too often organizations fight "bubble wars" for extended periods of time, trying to decide which partitioning is the best choice. Eventually the upper level bubbles become such conglomerates that their names can say little more than "Process <noun>."

Another problem with the data flow method is the size of the data dictionary. If five levels of diagrams exist, hundreds of data flow leveling equations may be required. Moreover, complex interfaces (with other systems, devices, and humans) tend to aggravate the data flow leveling equation problem, leading to project data dictionary "explosions" of 1000+ pages of dictionary documentation. (The authors have seen a number of large projects with this recurring problem.) CASE tools can help get all the syntax in shape. But the semantics, the underlying meaning, is beyond what any human reviewer can digest. So communication, most vital in analysis, is greatly weakened. Moreover, interfaces are volatile. The continual change for systems with complex interfaces causes even further syntactic and (more significant) semantic consistency problems.

The data flow approach still has a strong functional emphasis. And thus it is subject to the same change resiliency weaknesses that we discussed earlier.

The data flow approach has very weak data structure emphasis, and this is one of the greater concerns. The data flow diagram gives very weak emphasis to the data store. And this weakness is duly acknowledged by many authors describing the data flow method. So, many authors have tried to tie information modeling concepts into data flow diagramming to compensate for the weakness. It's an academically pleasing idea (two perspectives, one system under consideration). Yet even in books, the connection is very weak—for example, Yourdon, 1989, discusses the tie-in, but the leverage attainable in problem domain understanding from data modeling and its influence on a data flow model is all but ignored. And, more important than what a textbook says, *in practice the connection seems virtually non-existent.* On large projects that we have observed at several government contractors, as well as at a variety of business data processing organizations, the same pattern emerges again and again:

- The analysts rush off to do data flow diagrams.
- After a while, out of synch in time and content, another team works on an information model (this team is called the "database group").
- The second team gets great subject matter understanding.
- The first team likes the insight but resists the massive changes they must make (having grabbed for functionality first).
- The functional (DFD) team wins out, and the results of the two teams never get reconciled ("oh, we'll put it together in design").

Each analyst needs the benefit of both perspectives. *In practice, separate models keep critical issues too disjoint.* And although CASE tool support could help somewhat, the analyst with data flow diagrams works primarily with a model that hides the impact of the data structure.[6]

Another concern is that DFDs are not very helpful for systems or parts of systems that primarily update and retrieve data. Unlike the familiar transaction processing systems of the 1970s and early 1980s, most real-world systems today follow this pattern: the diagrams basically show a pair of bubbles, one bubble getting data and writing into a store, and one bubble pulling information out of that store and delivering the data. For example, an air traffic control system for the most part uses one bubble to dump in the data, and another bubble to later retrieve the data. Most of the system can be specified in this fashion. Pretty bubble-to-bubble-to-bubble textbook transformations are limited to fairly small aspects of the system, in which the processing is extensive enough to warrant such a refinement of data from one sub-step to the next and so on—for example, tracking calculations,

---

[6] Seeing this need again and again spurred us on to develop a single, multiple-layered notation for OOA; analysts can see the layers they want to see within one model, with the ability to view Subjects, Class-&-Objects, Structures, Attributes, and Services as a unified whole.

where tracking is a very important but rather small part when compared to the overall system to be analyzed and specified.

Another major concern about the data flow approach is moving to design: the double burden of shifting the underlying method of organization *and* adding implementation detail. This burden reminds the authors of the cartoon that shows a wide planning chart converging at one point, with a box reading "and then a miracle happens," followed by a wide path of planning charts emanating from the box. The transition from analysis to design has been a constant source of frustration. Many papers have been written; little progress has been made. It's tough enough to add implementation-based design considerations. Adding a substantial shift in underlying representation has made this transition an untenable problem. Data flows are a network representation of bubbles and stores; design-oriented structure charts are a hierarchical representation of modules. And no matter how many cute cartoons are drawn to depict the transition, the radical change in underlying representation causes a major chasm between analysis and design models. As Seidewitz argues in an unpublished paper [Seidewitz, 1989], "Functional analysis and specification techniques actually sacrifice closeness to the problem domain in order to allow a smooth transition to functional design methods."

A similar problem plagues those who have tried to follow structured analysis with object-oriented design; this trouble seems especially popular with those wrestling with Ada-oriented methods. However, if the object-oriented paradigm is so powerful as an underlying design perspective, why not apply those concepts as a foundation for improving analysis? This technique seems far more natural than many of the 10–100 page papers we have seen on such a transition, which in effect say, "Oh good. The analysts have done their structured analysis stuff. Let's pick the pieces of their results to get a first-cut, object-oriented view. Then on to the good stuff—design." This shift in underlying representation causes an even larger gap between analysis and design models. Such a gap is disastrous over time: requirements documents are ignored, continual changes in requirements are difficult to move into the design, and traceability—a *must* in Government system acquisition—is left with only form, and very little content.

For many years, analysts were stymied by the underlying representation shift as they moved from analysis to design. It prevented practitioners from systematically adding design-dependent detail to the results of analysis. Design should consist solely of expanding the requirements model to account for the complexities introduced in selecting a particular implementation—e.g., human-computer dialogue, task management, and data storage management. Problem domain constructs, such as Aircraft, should continue from analysis into design.

It's a matter of using the same underlying representation in analysis and design.

1.3.3 Information Modeling

Information modeling has evolved over a number of years. The primary modeling tool of information modeling—the entity-relationship diagram—has evolved into semantic data models. Modeling the world in data has helped capture problem domain content.

Here's an equation to help identify this method:

Information Modeling = Objects
+ Attributes
+ Relationships
+ Supertype/Sub-types
+ Associative Objects

Since the mid-70s, the information modeling discipline has used the term "object" in a very non-standard way, when examined against the use of the term over the centuries. As used within entity-relationship modeling (e.g., Chen, 1976), information modeling (e.g., Flavin, 1981), and semantic data modeling (e.g., Shlaer and Mellor, 1988), an "object" is a symbol which represents one or more occurrences of a real-world "entity."

Two strategies have been developed and applied. The older strategy says: Develop an indented list of attributes. Put the attributes into object buckets. Add relationships (mappings between occurrences). Refine with supertype/sub-types (to extract common attributes) and associative objects (to describe certain relationships). Then normalize (a step-by-step approach to reduce data redundancy, typically preparing for relational database implementation).

The newer strategy is much the same, except that the initial step is to find objects in the real world, and describe them with attributes. Otherwise, one proceeds in basically the same fashion.

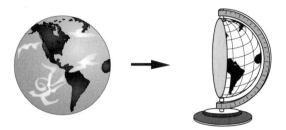

Figure 1.3: Information Modeling

With the newer strategy, information modeling maps directly from the problem domain to Objects in the model. This improvement in mapping is large, but a more detailed mapping is needed.

Information modeling is a partial method. It is well presented in several books (e.g., Shlaer and Mellor, 1988) and papers (e.g., Loomis, Shaw, Rumbaugh, 1987). Here is a list of missing concepts:

1. *Services:* the behavior, encapsulated and treated with the Attributes as an intrinsic whole.
2. *Messages:* a narrow, well-defined interface, depicting processing interdependency.
3. *Inheritance:* explicit representation of Attribute and Service commonality (more than just extracting common attributes into a supertype).
4. *Structure:* Generalization-Specialization and Whole-Part Structures, as fundamental human methods of organization, are not central issues (but should be).

1.3.4 An Observation on Stability vs. Volatility

Stability vs. volatility[7]—at issue is the impact of additions, extensions, changes, and deletions of features in the description of system requirements. This is especially important when considering "families" of systems—i.e., situations where a variety of implementations may be needed. Stability is also important throughout the *development* phase of a project, when over-optimistic goals need to be toned down from a full implementation (with adequate time, money, and people) to a lesser system—a phenomenon sometimes called "downsizing requirements."

Eventually one must address processes and sub-processes (functions/sub-functions). For example, Services will be needed to

---

[7] This is an extension of Bertrand Meyer's comments on volatility [Meyer, 1988].

create an Object, connect an Object to other Objects, calculate a result, and provide ongoing monitoring. Yet how much the players (client, management, and technical staff) decide to automate this time and how sophisticated the Services may be are both quite volatile; they are continually subject to the quadruple constraint—people, capabilities, schedule, and budget.

External interfaces are the next most likely components to change. How smart or dumb are the devices? What do other systems need from the system under consideration? What does this system need from others? What requests will the human make as he uses the system?

The next part likely to change includes the Attributes that describe items in the problem domain. Yet these changes tend to apply to a single "Class-&-Object" (*a shortened way of saying "a Class and the Objects in that Class"*), e.g., "Aircraft" and its Attributes, such as call number, serial number, location (latitude, longitude, altitude), and status.

The most stable aspects of a system, those which are least susceptible to potential change, are the Class-&-Objects which strictly depict the problem domain and the system's responsibilities within that domain. For example, whether one specifies a very low-budget or a very sophisticated air traffic control system, one will still have the same basic Class-&-Objects with which to organize the analysis and ultimately the specification: "Aircraft," "Controller," "Airspace," and the like. A more expensive system will have more Attributes for certain Class-&-Objects. Also, a more expensive version will have more elaborate interfaces for monitoring devices and other systems (and additional Class-&-Objects to model this). The more expensive system will have more sophisticated Services defined for each Class-&-Object (e.g., "Aircraft" with an automated tracking Service, "Aircraft.Track"). Also, the more expensive version may have some additional Class-&-Objects (e.g., a "Radar" Class-&-Object, with corresponding Attributes, plus Services such as "Radar.Interrogate"). Yet by and large, the very stable aspect of the system (Class-&-Objects in the problem domain) will remain the same across what potentially could be major changes in scope of a software requirements activity.[8]

So in terms of approach, it's not that an analyst does not specify Services; this designation must be done, regardless of the simplicity

[8] Of course, *all* systems are susceptible to change, and OOA systems are just as susceptible as any other. But with OOA, the impact of the change is more easily identified, bounded, and assessed.

or complexity of the system. It's what comes first, what predominates. The key to understanding problem domain lies in deciding what is the primary view and the overall organization, communicating that understanding, and ultimately specifying requirements. Underlying OOA is the idea of using encapsulation to hide the more volatile elements; with OOA, analysts base the overall structure of their thinking and specification on the more stable elements.

1.3.5 Object-Oriented

This section presents the basics, the principles, the approach, the motivations and benefits, and a multi-layer example.

The basics

Terminology. "Object-Oriented" is a difficult term, because the term "Object" has been used in different ways within two very different disciplines:

- From Information Modeling, meaning a representation of some real-world thing, and some number of occurrences of that thing.
- From Object-Oriented Programming Languages, meaning a run-time instance of some processing and values, defined by a static description called a "class."

Chapter 3 establishes definitions for both "object" and "class." An equation for recognizing an object-oriented approach is:

Object-Oriented = Classes and Objects

+ Inheritance

+ Communication with messages[9]

With this equation, one can look at different languages, environments, methods, and books and ask "Are they really object-oriented?" Unfortunately, many times the answer is "no"; object-oriented suffers from being a catchy marketing phrase, used at times to mean "the good stuff."

Is Ada an object-oriented language? Not today. Genericity (that is, typed parameters) is convenient, but no substitute for inheritance. At some point, Ada itself is likely to include classes, objects, and

---

[9] Communication with messages is a principle for managing complexity. Just because one programming language has a language construct called "message" (as in Smalltalk) and another has a language construct called "function" (as in C++) does not make either one more or less object-oriented.

inheritance. In the interim, Software Productivity Solutions of Melbourne, Florida markets ClassicAda™, a preprocessor which provides the missing object-oriented constructs.

Is Information Modeling object-oriented (e.g., *Object-Oriented Systems Analysis* [Shlaer and Mellor, 1988], a book better titled "Making Semantic Data Modeling Practical")? No. Its "objects" are data-only. Inheritance is missing. A uniform processing dependency mechanism is missing.

Merging of Disciplines. OOA builds upon the best concepts from Information Modeling, Object-Oriented Programming Languages, and Knowledge-Based Systems—*the concepts which have a solid basis in underlying principles for managing complexity.*

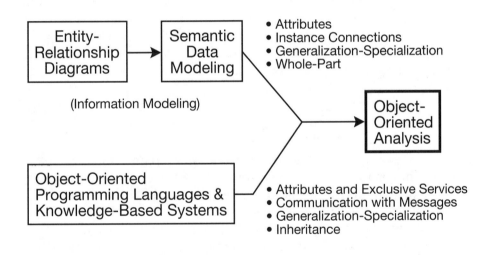

Figure 1.4: Merging of disciplines

From Information Modeling come constructs analogous to Attributes, Instance Connections, Generalization-Specialization, and Whole-Part. From Object-Oriented Programming Languages and Knowledge-Based Systems come the encapsulation of Attributes and exclusive Services, communication with messages, Generalization-Specialization, and Inheritance.

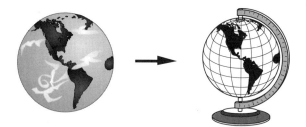

Figure 1.5: Object-Oriented

A direct mapping. OOA directly maps problem domain and system responsibility directly into a model.

Instead of an indirect mapping from problem domain to function/sub-function or problem domain to flows and bubbles, the mapping is direct, from the problem domain to the model, e.g., Owner, Vehicle, LegalEvent, and Clerk.

When OOA may not be helpful. OOA is not very helpful for systems with very limited responsibilities, or for systems with only one or two Class-&-Objects.

For example, if a system takes an input stream, runs a ten page algorithm on it, and produces an output stream, then just a flowchart, a list of equations, and some terse text would be sufficient. The system's responsibilities are very limited.

As another example, consider a system which manages a collection of one Class and the Objects in that Class. With only one or two OOA Class-&-Objects, the overall partitioning is not very exciting. However, the discipline of defining Attributes and Services would be very helpful. Yet the system has only one or two Class-&-Objects.

Don't be quick to assume that your system falls in a category where OOA is not helpful. For example, consider an aircraft simulation system. A traditional approach would be to build a single, gigantic event-driven simulation (a big algorithm, not well-partitioned). Yet an object-oriented approach partitions the system into parallel subsystems (electrical, mechanical, hydraulic, and the like); each subsystem follows a similar pattern; and each subsystem has many Class-&-Objects.

The principles

OOA is based on the uniform application of the principles for managing complexity:

1 Abstraction
   a Procedural
   b Data
2 Encapsulation
3 Inheritance
4 Association
5 Communication with messages
6 Pervading methods of organization
   a Objects and attributes
   b Whole and parts
   c Classes and members, and distinguishing
     between them
7 Scale
8 Categories of behavior
   a Immediate causation
   b Change over time
   c Similarity of functions

Figure 1.6: Principles for managing complexity
(with reference numbers, used in the tables which follow)

This table presents the differences between the various analysis methods, assessed in the light of principles for managing complexity:

Methods	1a	1b	2	3	4	5	6a	6b	6c	7	8a	8b	8c
Functional Decomposition	x												
Data Flow	x									x	x		
Information Modeling					x		x	x	x				
Object-Oriented	x	x	x	x	x	x	x	x	x	x	x	x	x

Principles of Managing Complexity

Figure 1.7: Analysis methods and the principles they incorporate

The table summarizes the OOA constructs which utilize these principles:

Principles for Managing Complexity

OOA Construct	1a	1b	2	3	4	5	6a	6b	6c	7	8a	8b	8c
Class-&-Object		X	X				X						
Gen-Spec Structure			X					X					
Whole-Part Structure								X					
Attribute		X	X	X			X		X				
Service	X	X	X	X					X		X	X	X
Instance Connection				X									
Message Connection			X		X						X		
Subject							X		X				

Figure 1.8: OOA's application of principles for managing complexity

The approach

In an overall approach, OOA consists of five major activities:

Finding Class-&-Objects
Identifying Structures
Identifying Subjects
Defining Attributes
Defining Services[10,11]

These are indeed *activities*, not sequential steps. The activities guide the analyst from high levels of abstraction (e.g., problem-domain Class-&-Objects) to increasingly lower levels of abstraction (Structures, Attributes, and Services). And the ordering of these five activities represents the most common *overall* approach.

At MCC (Austin, Texas), researchers have observed that analysts/designers tend to work at a higher level of abstraction, then see a detailed area, dive into it, investigate it, and return to a higher level

---

[10] Note that we are applying one of the methods of organization which pervades all human thinking—whole and part—in order to better communicate OOA itself!

[11] To specially set apart the terms Class-&-Object, Structure, Subject, Attribute, and Service, we capitalize the words whenever they are used throughout this book.

of abstraction. In fact, we've seen the same thing with our children. And we've observed the same pattern as analysts apply OOA. Upon finding a Class-&-Object (e.g., Radar), some analysts want to add in a Service name (e.g., "I know I need SearchForAirborneItem in here."). So they write that Service name down on the Service layer, and then continue looking for another problem domain Class-&-Object.

It's helpful as a general pattern to move from one activity to the next, but it's not mandatory. In fact, some analysts prefer to go from Class-&-Objects to Attributes to Structures to Services; others prefer to go from Class-&-Objects to Services to Structures to Attributes. And this is fine; these are indeed activities.

For more complex problem domains, the analyst may add a Subject layer to guide readers through a larger model and partition work packages.

The OOA model is presented and reviewed in five layers:

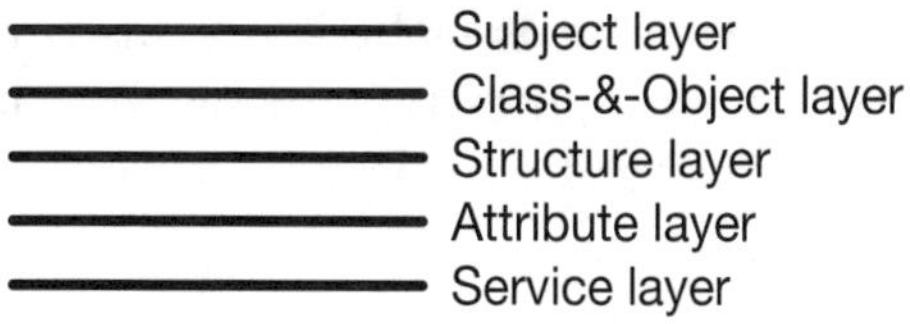

———————————— Subject layer
———————————— Class-&-Object layer
———————————— Structure layer
———————————— Attribute layer
———————————— Service layer

Figure 1.9: The multi-layer model

These five layers are much like overlapping pieces of clear plastic (i.e., transparencies) which gradually present more and more detail.

Deciding when the analysis and specification is complete is domain-driven, system-responsibility-driven, and checklist-driven[12] —within the context of schedule and budget constraints.

The motivations and benefits

Why OOA? Seven prime motivations and benefits:

1. *Tackle more challenging problem domains.* OOA brings extra emphasis to the understanding of problem domains.

---

[12] Such a quality checklist may include strategy checks (summarized in Appendix A) and model consistency checks (included in Chapter 8).

2. *Improve analyst and problem domain expert interaction.* OOA organizes analysis and specification using the methods of organization
which pervade people's thinking.

3. *Increase the internal consistency of analysis results.* OOA reduces the
bandwidth between different analysis activities, by treating Attributes and Services as an intrinsic whole.

4. *Explicitly represent commonality.* OOA uses inheritance to identify
and capitalize on commonality of Attributes and Services.

5. *Build specifications resilient to change.* OOA packages volatility
within problem-domain constructs, providing stability over
changing requirements and similar systems.

6. *Reuse analysis results,* accommodating both families of systems and
practical tradeoffs within a system. OOA organizes results based
upon problem domain constructs, for present reuse and for future
reuse.

7. *Provide a consistent underlying representation* for analysis (what is to
be built) and design (how it is to be built this time). OOA establishes a continuum of representation, for systematically expanding
analysis results into a specific design.

A multi-layer example

An example based on a motor vehicle registration application
follows. This example lets you peek ahead; the notation and strategy
for building these layers are presented in Chapters 3 to 7.

1. People

2. Legal

Figure 1.10: An OOA example—Subject layer

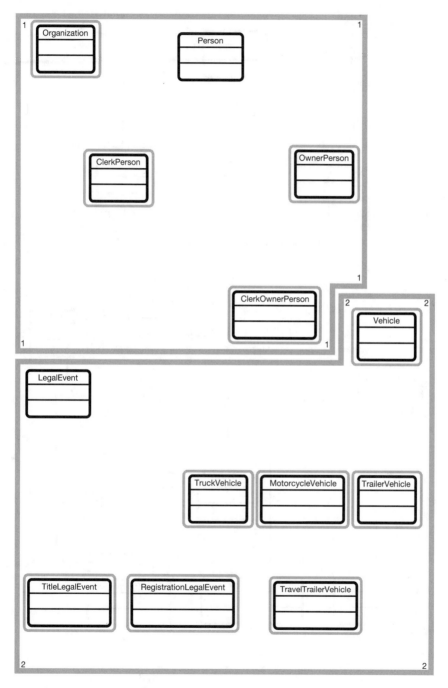

Figure 1.11: An OOA example—Subject and Class-&-Object layers

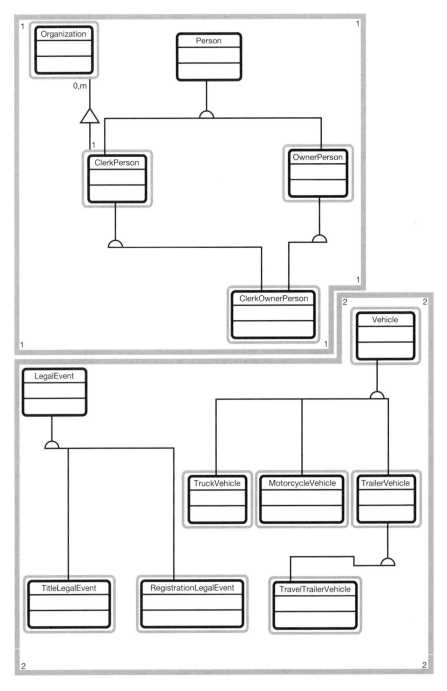

Figure 1.12: An OOA example—Subject, Class-&-Object, and Structure layers

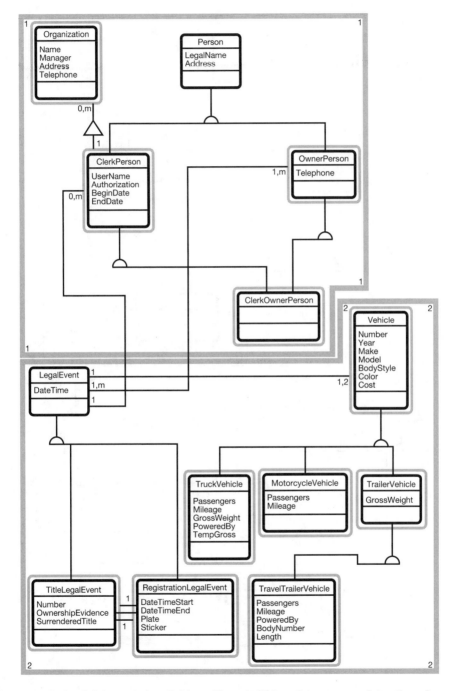

Figure 1.13: An OOA example—Subject, Class-&-Object, Structure, and Attribute layers

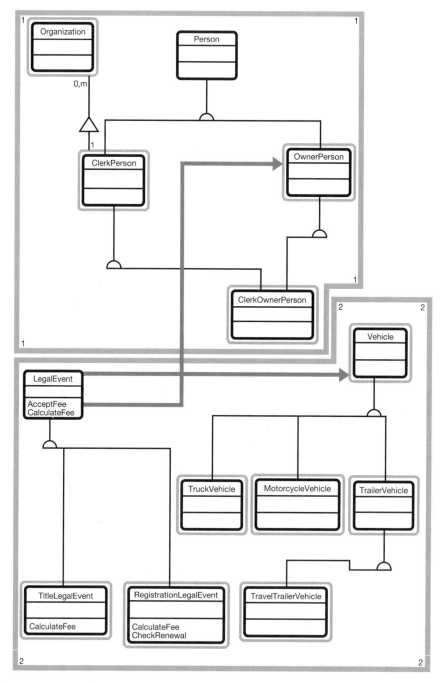

Figure 1.14: An OOA example—Subject, Class-&-Object, Structure, and Service layers

2

Experiencing an
Object Perspective

This chapter addresses some very specific concepts of object-orientedness. To drive the concepts home experientially, we use the language Smalltalk as a convenient vehicle of communication. This usage does not suggest that Smalltalk itself is an OOA tool or that one *must* use an object-oriented programming language in order to practice OOA (although prototypes and demonstration programs used to better understand requirements could be built from OOA models using Smalltalk). Rather, the chapter uses Smalltalk, a fully object-oriented language and environment, to elucidate certain critical aspects that are object-oriented.

In 1987, the U.S. Naval Weapons Center asked one of the authors to conduct a one-week workshop on Object-Oriented Software Engineering. They wanted to explore what was so important about this approach; in effect, they asked: *what's the big deal about object-oriented anything?*

So we began to investigate the underlying object-oriented principles that could be applied to programming languages, then to design, and finally to analysis. We spent the first three days immersing ourselves in a fully object-oriented language and environment: Smalltalk. We executed many, many Smalltalk examples. *Everything* in Smalltalk is object-oriented, so one gets fully immersed in an object-oriented world.

Similarly, we recommend that you, the reader, take the time to explore Smalltalk. For this exploration, we recommend Smalltalk/V® from Digitalk, Inc. (El Segundo, California USA); their family of products run on a variety of platforms, including IBM compatibles (running DOS, Windows, or OS/2) and Macintosh; the software is reasonably priced and comes with over 200 ready-to-run examples. Although in a different price range, products from Parc Place Systems (Mountain View, California USA) also are worth considering.[1]

---

[1] This is not intended as an absolute endorsement of hardware platforms or different versions of Smalltalk. It is a recommendation in terms of cost-effective learning tools.

By working through a series of graduated examples, you can work first-hand with a fully object-oriented language and environment. The experience is worthwhile, even for those who no longer write programs for a living.

The end of this chapter focuses on the key points for us as requirements analysts, preparing to apply OOA in day-to-day work.

2.1 SMALLTALK

Welcome to Smalltalk, a fully object-oriented language and environment.

In Smalltalk, everything is based on objects. For example, integers are objects, panes (i.e., sub-areas of a display window) are objects, and even the language syntax itself consists of objects. And together with objects comes the notion of sending messages to objects to get things done.

This fully object-oriented arena captures a fundamentally different perspective than the one most programmers are familiar with. The following sections will delve into it with examples of Smalltalk objects, methods, messages, classes, and inheritance.

2.2 SMALLTALK OBJECTS

A Smalltalk object is an encapsulation of information and the description of its manipulation. It has private variables and corresponding methods that can be performed on those variables. In other words, an object has data (state) inside, and knows what to do with that data.

4

Figure 2.1: An integer object

This figure is a representation of an integer object, with the value 4. The variables and methods are treated as an intrinsic whole. And the interface is kept very narrow—the only way to manipulate the variables is by using visible methods.

'this is fun'

Figure 2.2: A string object

This object is a string object. It not only has the data structure "this is fun" hidden inside it, but also knows what actions are appropriate for the variables inside. The object knows, for example, that it is meaningless to compute the square root of "this is fun," but it is meaningful to compute the length of the string and return the result as an integer.

```
#( 7 6 5 4 3 )
```

Figure 2.3: An array of objects

This object is an array of objects (here the objects in the array all happen to be integer objects). And the object shown in Figure 2.3 knows what to do with its internal variables, and what actions are pertinent to arrays of objects.

```
aPane
```

Figure 2.4: A pane object

This object is more sophisticated. It's an object that corresponds to a window on a display device. It hides variables inside, and knows the actions that are appropriate for panes.

2.3 SMALLTALK MESSAGES

A Smalltalk message tells an object what to do.
    A message says:

> Here's the object that gets the message
>   (called the "receiver object").
> Here's the method I want done now
>   (called the "method selector").
> Here are the arguments to use.

The operation is named in the message, but what is done is actually hidden (encapsulated) in the object that receives the message.
    A Smalltalk message is a selection of one of the manipulations that an object knows how to perform. A message says "do this one," and the object itself knows what actions to carry out in response.
    This perspective is fundamentally different from the *procedural* perspective almost all software engineers learned in their introduc-

tory programming courses. When first using Smalltalk, many try to map messages into a familiar function or procedure-call format. But the mapping is hard to maintain. So after a while, one begins to think of objects as strong encapsulations of data and processing on that data; when a message is sent to the object, the object does its thing, and then a response is received from the object.

Some examples follow.

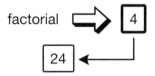

Figure 2.5: The factorial example

In this example, the message "factorial" is sent to an integer object. Hidden inside the object is its current value, 4. The message tells the object what to do. The object has a corresponding method describing what it is to do upon receipt of the message. Notice the strong encapsulation of data and the processing on that data. The object with the value 4 does its work, and then returns the result (which is itself an object)—an integer object with the value 24. So what it means to "compute factorial" is hidden inside the object; the interface between the object and other objects is specified with visible methods; and the means for getting things done is sending messages to invoke methods.

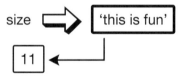

Figure 2.6: The size example

In this example, the message "size" is being sent to a string object. The object knows what to do upon receipt of such a message, and it sends back a result (which happens to be an integer object).

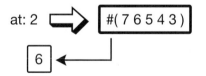

Figure 2.7: An example with an array object

This third example involves an object with a little more sophistication—it's an array object. It understands messages pertinent to its variables. The message sent to the object is "at: two" (read as "at two" by some, and "at colon two" by others), which is a method selector and one argument. The object does its work, and returns an integer object with the value 6 as the result.

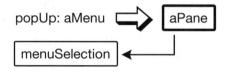

Figure 2.8: A pane object

The fourth example hides even more elaborate data and processing on that data. The message "popUp: aMenu" is sent, meaning "here's the method (popUp) I want you to invoke and here's the argument you'll need (aMenu)." The object does all of the work of putting up the pop-up menu, getting a valid selection, removing the pop-up menu, and returning an object containing the menu selection.

2.4 SMALLTALK CLASSES

In addition to objects and messages, Smalltalk has classes. All object-oriented programming languages have such mechanisms. In Smalltalk, it's a mechanism for *class*ifying variables and methods according to their similarities and special-case extensions.

Smalltalk classes express static descriptions of data and methods. Objects are run-time instances of a class. For example, the "Integer" class defines the hidden variables and the methods that apply to integers. At run time, a programmer can create an object of a class, give it a value (via a message) and start doing things with it (again via messages).

Consider two Smalltalk class examples.

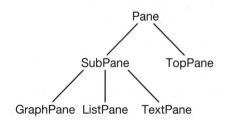

Figure 2.9: An example of Smalltalk classes

A pane is a window sub-area in a display device. A pane can be specialized into a SubPane (which knows about scroll bars) and a TopPane (which is responsible for an entire window). A SubPane is further specialized (extended) into a GraphPane (with variables and methods for graphics), a ListPane (with variables and methods for list manipulation and item selection), and a TextPane (with variables and methods for text editing). Observe that the classes organize the definition of variables and methods according to their similarities at a higher level, and then extend or specialize those variables and methods at lower levels.

Collection	contain a number of objects
Bag	collection of unordered elements in which duplicates are allowed
Indexed Collection	collection with index
Fixed Size Collection	fixed indexable sequence
Array	fixed indexable sequence of objects
ByteArray	fixed indexable sequence of bytes
String	fixed indexable sequence of characters
Symbol	unique fixed size sequence of characters
Ordered Collection	collection which can grow
Sorted Collection	collection sorted by instantiated compare code
Set	unordered collection of unique objects
Dictionary	collection of unique key & value pairs
SymbolSet	collection of unique fixed size sequences of chars

Figure 2.10: Another example of Smalltalk classes

The second example of Smalltalk classes also illustrates the theme of generalization-specialization, this time with some lower level variables and methods. Remember that everything in Smalltalk is set up with classes—it's where the variables and methods are defined. So, again, observe the hierarchical patterning of general to specific, or of basic capability to extension of that capability.

For an object-oriented programming language, tools are needed to browse a class hierarchy—it may end up being five or more levels deep, and may consist of 200 or more classes. With such depth of classes, browsing tools are needed so that the "ripple effect" of a change at a higher level can be controlled on lower levels.[2] Usually this type of control means displaying a class on the screen, along with its inherited variables and methods; this area is one of continued

[2] The number of classes in the OOA modeling domain is dependent upon the complexity of the problem domain, and the system's responsibilities in that context. This results in much fewer classes than one might use in an object-oriented programming language like Smalltalk.

research. (However, such tools are not needed for OOA; in practice, Gen-Spec Structures rarely exceed three levels).

2.5 SMALLTALK INHERITANCE

Hand-in-hand with Smalltalk classes comes Smalltalk inheritance.

Inheritance is a mechanism that simplifies the definition of software components that are similar to those previously defined.

The benefit of inheritance in an object-oriented programming language is that a designer/implementer can say, "Yes, I want to reuse what you've got there, except that I want to add these variables, and add to or extend the processing in this fashion. It's just like this, but a little bit different." This attitude is vastly different than, and worlds apart from, saying, "OK. So this is what you built. And I've got to use it as-is, or else go off and write my own."

Inheritance is a significant mechanism for reuse, and for explicitly capturing commonality. It consists of four major aspects:

1. For each class, the class inherits the variables defined in its superclass(es) (those classes above it, working up through the hierarchy).

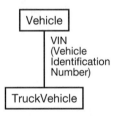

Figure 2.11: Inheriting variables

For example, Vehicle Identification Number (VIN) is defined for Vehicle, and inherited by TruckVehicle.

2. For each class, the class inherits the methods defined in its superclass(es).

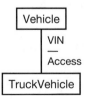

Figure 2.12: Inheriting methods

For example, Access is defined for Vehicle, and inherited by TruckVehicle.

3. For each class, the class can add variables.

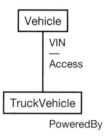

Figure 2.13: Adding variables

For example, PoweredBy is defined as applicable to a TruckVehicle, but not to all vehicles.

4. For each class, the class can add or extend inherited methods.

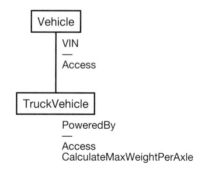

Figure 2.14: Adding and extending/overriding methods

For example, Access is defined for Vehicle, and then extended/ overridden for TruckVehicle; CalculateMaxWeightPerAxle is defined for TruckVehicle, but not for all vehicles.

Thus, the bottom-line benefit of inheritance is that it gives us a basis for explicitly capturing commonality of variables and exclusive methods on those variables.

Here are some inheritance examples from Smalltalk:

```
Pane                    menu, pop-up, font—for a window sub-area
   SubPane              scroll bar
      GraphPane         bitmap
                        basic graphics tool (lines)
   ListPane             indexed collection of strings
   TextPane             strings
                        display, scroll, edit (append, search & replace)
   TopPane              color, border, frame, label
                        (a pane responsible for an entire window)
```

Figure 2.15: An example of Smalltalk inheritance

Panes know about variables and methods pertinent to a window sub-area, and the corresponding menus, pop-ups, and fonts; Sub-Panes add capability, with knowledge of the variables and methods pertinent to scroll bars hidden inside; GraphPanes carry the variables and methods even further, with a hidden bitmap and graphics tools; and so on.

Note the generalization (commonality) at higher levels, followed by the extension in special cases at lower levels, all expressed succinctly with inheritance. Effectively, you see an elaboration of variables and processing sophistication as you work your way down the hierarchy.

```
Collection                add,...
   Bag                     add,...
   Indexed Collection      ...
      Fixed Size Collection  add,...
      Array                 ...
      ByteArray             ...
      String                edit,...
      Symbol                ...
   Ordered Collection      add,...
      Sorted Collection    add,...
   Set    ...
   Dictionary              add,...
   SymbolSet               add,...
```

Figure 2.16: Another example of Smalltalk inheritance

The second example illustrates how one method, "add," gets extended again and again as one moves down the hierarchy. New methods can be added at whatever level is appropriate, e.g., the "edit" method shown in the example.[3]

---

[3] Just as in real life, a child may know or do more than his ancestors!

2.6 KEY POINTS

So what are the key lessons to be extracted from this small taste of Smalltalk[4]?

1. Variables and exclusive methods on the variables are treated as an intrinsic whole.
2. The interface between objects is fully defined by the methods that are visible to other objects. The only way one can access or manipulate the values hidden inside an object is by sending a message to an object, corresponding to a method defined for that object.
3. Classes and inheritance provide ways to model a problem domain and explicitly depict generalization-specialization of variables and methods.

2.7 TERMINOLOGY MAP

At this introductory stage, we feel it would be helpful to introduce a "terminology map," specifically for those readers already familiar with object-oriented programming languages or semantic data modeling. *Our rationale is to select a consistent set of terms that are descriptive in the context of analysis and specification, but that do not imply a particular implementation technology* (e.g., the choice of a programming language).

Semantic Data modeling	OOPLs	OOA (second edition)
Object	Class	Class
Attribute	Variable	Attribute
—	Method	Service
Occurrence	Object (Instance)	Object (Instance)
Supertype/subtype	Superclass/subclass	Gen-Spec Structure
Aggregation	—	Whole-Part Structure
Relationship	—	Instance Connection
—	Message	Message Connection

[4] In a study of programming languages, additional points are significant, such as the need for dynamic binding. However, this chapter focuses just on those aspects of Smalltalk which illuminate concepts pertinent to OOA.

INTRODUCTION TO CHAPTERS 3–7

The chapters that follow cover the five major activities of OOA. Each chapter is structured into four sections:

- What
- Why
- How
- Key Points

The "Key Points" sections wrap up each chapter, with

- Notation
- Strategy
- Example—Sensor System
- Example—Registration and Title System
- Example—Real-Time Airlift System

3

Finding Class-&-Objects

The objects are just there for the picking. [Meyer, 1988]

Nuts! Pertinent Class-&-Objects within a problem domain and within the context of a system's responsibilities are rarely "just there for the picking."

As analysts experienced in applying OOA across widely divergent problem domains, we recognize certain patterns across systems. And so at times it might seem that the Class-&-Objects are "just there for the picking." But in fact we are applying specific points of strategy, which are described in this chapter and supplemented by the strategies in the chapters which follow.

This chapter presents specific guidelines for finding Class-&-Objects. We begin by defining what we mean by "class" and "object," and then describe why they play such an important role in the analysis and specification of a system. The meat of the chapter includes *notation; where to look* for Class-&-Objects; *what to look for*; and *what to consider and challenge*.

3.1 CLASS-&-OBJECTS—WHAT

"Object" and "class" are words with meanings established over thousands of years.

> Object. [something thrown in the way (Medieval Latin), a casting before (Latin)] A person or thing to which action, thought, or feeling is directed. Anything visible or tangible; a material product or substance.
>
> Class. [a division of the Roman people (Latin); a calling, summons (Greek)] A number of people or things grouped together because of certain likenesses or common traits.
> [Webster's, 1977]

In OOA, these terms need to reflect both the "problem domain" and the "system's responsibilities":

> Problem Domain. A field of endeavor under consideration.

System's Responsibilities. An arrangement of things accountable for, related together as a whole.

For example:

A problem domain might include...	Yet a system's responsibilities within that domain may only include...
Person	Person
Name	Name
Address	Address
Height	
Weight	
Age	
Consumer habits	
Lifestyle choices	
Religious affiliation	
•••	

Figure 3.1: Problem domain and the system's responsibilities

With OOA, an analyst *studies* the overall problem domain, *filters* that problem domain understanding to just those aspects which are within the system's responsibilities, and *models* it accordingly.

And so for OOA, the terms "object" and "class" are defined reflecting both the problem domain and the system's responsibilities:

Object. An *abstraction* of something in a problem domain, reflecting the capabilities of a system to keep information about it, interact with it, or both; an *encapsulation* of Attribute values and their exclusive Services. (synonym: an Instance)

Class. A description of one or more Objects with a uniform set of Attributes and Services, including a description of how to create new Objects in the Class.

Class-&-Object. A term meaning *"a Class and the Objects in that Class."*

3.2 CLASS-&-OBJECTS—WHY

The primary motivation for identifying Class-&-Objects is to match the technical representation of a system more closely to the conceptual view of the real world.

Abstracting problem domain Class-&-Objects affects understandability and effective communication. Analysts first must understand the problem domain at hand; it makes little sense to run off and start writing air traffic control functional requirements, without first studying, expressing, and validating our understanding of what air traffic control is really all about. Defining Class-&-Objects as an abstraction of the real world helps us gain and communicate significant problem domain understanding—applicable for the system under consideration, and with a view toward reusable analysis results. All of this we document in the form of an OOA model. Ultimately this single model consists of five layers (Subject, Class-&-Object, Structure, Attribute, and Service), produced during the five major activities of OOA.

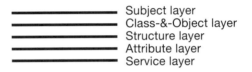

Figure 3.2: A multi-layer model

These five layers are much like overlapping pieces of clear plastic (i.e., transparencies) which are used to gradually present more and more detail.

Another motivation for emphasizing Class-&-Objects is our desire to create a stable framework for analysis and specification. The Class-&-Objects in an air traffic control system today will probably be the same as the Class-&-Objects in an air traffic control system five years from now—but the Attributes and Services for the Objects in those Classes may change radically. Class-&-Objects are relatively stable over time, and provide a basis for moving over time towards reusable analysis results. Problem-domain-based encapsulation helps reduce volatility and subsequent re-work, structuring the overall analysis and specification strategy upon a framework that is likely to be much more stable over time:

Interfaces between system components—highly volatile

Functions—very volatile

Sequencing of functions—very volatile

Data, held over time—less volatile

Problem Domain Class-&-Objects—the least volatile

Moreover, the encapsulation of Attributes and exclusive Services forms the basis for treating the Attributes and corresponding Services as an intrinsic whole. Analysts focus on an Object's state (data) and behavior (processing) *together*. Separating process analysis from data analysis is not even a consideration—both must be considered as an intrinsic whole.

The OOA model also provides a basis for an initial expression of the system *context*. Context is not defined by a diagram, drawn by a systems analyst making a technical decision. Rather, clients, managers, analysts, competitors, government regulators, and standards bearers all affect the system context over time. System context is an indication of how much of the problem domain will be embraced by the automated system, what data will be held over time, and how much processing sophistication will be included—all within the "quadruple constraint" (inspired by Rosenau, 1981) that affects all systems:

Quadruple Constraint = Capability + Schedule + Budget + People

System context is set by quadruple constraint negotiations. To control a project, a manager must be accountable in all four areas. (Perhaps you've known highly acclaimed managers who were always fine on budget and schedule, but were never held accountable for the content (capability) of their delivered results.) All four aspects must be managed effectively.

Class-&-Objects represent the initial expression of context. And the subsequent OOA activities provide an increasingly detailed description of the context in terms of Structures, Attributes, and Services.

A final motivation for identifying Class-&-Objects is to avoid shifting the underlying representation as we move from systems analysis to design. The gap, or "twilight zone," between analysis and design seemed impenetrable throughout the 1970s and 1980s: people have pondered the subject, drawn cartoons, and presented papers at seminars and conferences. Yet shifting from an underlying network organization for analysis (data flow diagrams) to an underlying hierarchical organization for design (structure charts) has been too magical for most practitioners and nearly always untraceable (a key issue of concern on large, critical systems). And recent attempts to transform an underlying network organization for analysis (data flow diagrams) to an underlying Object representation for design have met the same problem. The heart of design is taking the requirements and adding implementation detail to them—and that job is challenging enough. Throwing in a change in underlying representation has been the root cause of the analysis/design chasm.

We can resolve this dilemma by using an object-oriented representation in analysis, design, and implementation (using an object-oriented programming language is not required in applying OOA or OOD, but significant during implementation, maintenance, and reuse).

3.3 CLASS-&-OBJECTS—HOW

The strategy comes from practice and experience in the field, based upon Class-&-Objects found initially, as well as ones found later (and investigating why they were missed earlier). The strategy consists of notation, followed by where to look, what to look for, and what to consider and challenge.

3.3.1 Notation

The "Class-&-Object" symbol represents a Class and its Objects.

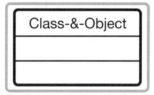

Figure 3.3: The OOA "Class-&-Object" symbol

The symbol represents both a Class (represented by the bold rounded rectangle, divided into three horizontal sections) and its Object(s) (represented by the light rectangle). Certain OOA connections map an Object to another[1]; other OOA connections map a Class to another[2]; other OOA connections map an Object to a Class.[3] This notation facilitates the explicit representation of such mappings. When using paper and pencil, just a simple rounded rectangle works fine. But with CASE tool support, the "Class-&-Object" symbol, with its separate rounded rectangles, makes explicit whether an attached line applies to the Class or to an Object.

The symbol is labeled with its Class name, Attribute(s) (appli-

[1] Namely, Whole-Part Structures, Instance Connections, and most Message Connections. These are discussed in Chapters 4, 6, and 7, respectively.

[2] Namely, Generalization-Specialization (Gen-Spec) Structures and certain Message Connections. These are discussed in Chapters 4 and 7, respectively.

[3] Namely, certain Message Connections, as discussed in Chapter 7.

cable to each Object in the Class), and Service(s) (applicable to each Object in the Class).

The Class name is a singular noun, or adjective and noun. A Class-&-Object name should describe a single Object within the Class—e.g., when each Object describes something that gets shipped, use "Shipment Item" (each Object is one item) rather than "Shipment" (which would describe an entire shipment, e.g., a truckload or plane load).

Choose Class-&-Object names using standard vocabulary for the subject matter. Stick with names the client is comfortable with. As we learned on an air traffic control system, switching to more semantically accurate terminology only frustrates the client. We replaced terms such as "Minimum Safe Altitude Warning" with "Aircraft-to-Airspace Conflict Alert," a "better" description of what was being described. Each time we used our terms, we could almost see the client mapping them into more familiar terminology. And every time he spoke, he used his terms, along with "or whatever it is you're calling it." Lesson learned: stick to standard vocabulary for the subject matter.

Use readable names. Everyday uppercase and lowercase conventions make names easier to read. Resist the urge to add prefix and suffix codes; they're a bother to read and troublesome when they change midstream. Sometimes prefixes are added to help group related names together for lists. But this convention is not needed in OOA. Attributes and Services are named within the context of a Class-&-Object, and are specified in the corresponding Class-&-Object specification.

One can think of a Class-&-Object symbol as a Class with one or more Objects in the Class, picturing it something like this:

Figure 3.4: Picturing some number of Objects within a Class

A variation on the "Class-&-Object" symbol is the "Class" symbol:[4]

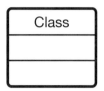

Figure 3.5: The OOA "Class" symbol

This symbol is used to represent a generalization Class from the problem domain, whose corresponding Objects are portrayed by its specializations which have Class-&-Object symbols. This symbol will come into active use once we reach Chapter 4.

Concerning the number of Classes in an OOA model: it's dependent upon the breadth and depth of the problem domain, and the system's responsibilities within it. 35 Classes is average; 110 Classes is large; and for problem domains with several problem sub-domains (e.g., air traffic control), there might be four or five problem sub-domains, with 50–100 Classes in each.

3.3.2 Where to Look

Investigate the problem domain: observe first-hand; listen actively; check previous OOA results; check other systems; read, read, read; and prototype.

Study the problem domain itself—the field of endeavor under consideration. This examination involves investing some time in investigative research.

Observe first-hand. Go for first-hand observation. Sit with an overloaded air traffic controller for an entire shift. Fly an F-18 flight simulator. Strive to get an intuitive feel for the challenges and frustrations your client faces; put yourself in his shoes and stay there a while. Especially for systems with humans in the loop, this is critical.

Actively listen to problem domain experts. Get in contact with problem domain experts; such an expert may be a master, guru, specialist, or veteran in the problem domain under consideration. *Actively* listen to problem domain experts—listen, digest, play back your understanding to them, and keep asking follow-up questions.

---

[4] Sometimes this is referred to as an "abstract" class.

Ask them to talk about the domain—what makes it interesting, what is most important (and why), what scenarios are most significant (and why). Note: you need access to problem domain experts; recruit your own, or get time commitments from ones in a client organization. Ideally, the initial analysis team consists of 3 super-analysts and 3 problem domain experts (odd numbers help when it's time to vote!).

Check previous OOA results. Check previous OOA results in the same and similar problem domains. Which Class-&-Objects can be directly reused? What lessons can be learned for finding Class-&-Objects pertinent to the system under consideration?

Check other systems. Similarly, check other systems in the same and similar problem domains. What lessons can be learned for finding Class-&-Objects pertinent to the system under consideration?

Read, read, read. Read the "requesting document." The client may supply some form of "requesting document," a description ranging in length from several sentences up to several reams. Identify the purpose (mission) and critical success factors for the system under consideration.

Ask the client for a concise summary of, say, 25, 50, or even 100 pages about the problem domain.

Go to *Encyclopaedia Britannica*'s *Macropaedia* for a 10–12 page professionally-written description of the problem domain under consideration; this is an excellent way to learn the terminology and fundamentals of a topic, set within a wider context than the system under consideration—e.g., air traffic control.

Check the US Library of Congress (or comparable) Subject Classification System (available in print, or even better, on CD-ROM) [Library of Congress, 1990]. It presents topics, along with corresponding broader topics and narrower topics, forming a lattice of potential Class-&-Objects. For problem domains which have been written about, it's a valuable source for rapid identification of potential Classes-&-Objects.

Scan whatever you can get your hands on, and set aside those sections that especially illuminate the subject matter and deserve detailed study and consideration. During an ongoing OOA consultation, a client told one of the authors to read a best-selling novel, *Red Phoenix* by Larry Bond (Warner Books, 1989), to learn how fighter aircraft are actually used (with the comment that the novel was just as accurate and much more concise than official government documents!). He was right; problem domain experts seemed a bit surprised at the depth of questions that the author asked during the next working session.

As you read, consider the nouns and draw pictures; these words will often give you a clue to potential Class-&-Objects in the system. This doesn't mean that you should simply circle the nouns and declare them Class-&-Objects (as some writers have proposed). Real systems are not that simple to analyze; more extensive strategies are needed. Read extensively, consider the nouns, and weigh them against the criteria presented later in this chapter, in "What to Look For" and "What to Consider and Challenge."

Follow through with more pictures. Collect any pictures you can—block diagrams, interface diagrams, system component diagrams, very high level data and/or control flow diagrams. In addition, draw plenty of your own pictures, using icons and lines between them, as initial sketches of the problem domain and how the pieces interact with each other.

Such investigative research pays off handsomely in rapidly gaining a broader perspective of the problem domain at hand.

Prototype.   Prototyping is essential for effective analysis—especially for systems with human-computer interaction.

Prototypes move requirements from being less *prescriptive* to being more *descriptive*. And good commercial tools are readily available for such prototyping.

Expectations of a client must be managed—it's not the product, it's not the product, it's not the product. But that is not a reason to leave out prototyping.

Summary.   In investigating the problem domain, observe firsthand; listen actively; check previous OOA results; check other systems; read, read, read; and prototype.

3.3.3   What to Look For

To find potential Class-&-Objects, look for: structures, other systems, devices, things or events remembered, roles played, operational procedures, sites, and organizational units. The items discussed here are presented in the order of most fruitful Class-&-Object finders first.

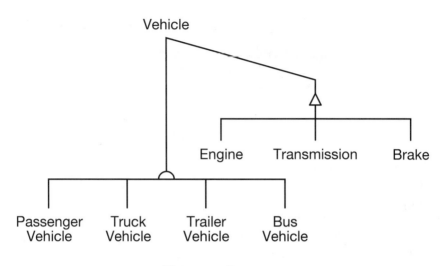

Figure 3.6: Structure

Structures. Structure is so significant for finding Class-&-Objects and representing problem domain complexity that it has its own activity in the OOA method. (Identifying Structure, the next activity in the OOA method, is discussed in Chapter 4.) Generalization-Specialization Structures and Whole-Part Structures are most fruitful; they bring strong intellectual leverage to the table. We will discuss both forms of structure in detail in Chapter 4.

Figure 3.7: Other system

Other systems. What other system or "external terminator" will the system under consideration interact with? This interaction could be hard-wired (e.g., with a cabled external system), transmission interaction (e.g., with an auto-altitude-reporting aircraft), or a result of human-computer interaction (e.g., a user-described vehicle).

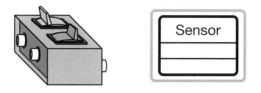

Figure 3.8: Device

Devices. What devices will the system under study need to interact with? Some devices may exchange data and control information with the system.

Do not add implementation-specific computer components (e.g., disk drives and display terminals); defer such considerations, keeping notes in a folder until the design phase of the project. You'll keep the requirements simpler this way, and avoid major re-work when the "unchangeable" computer components suddenly change on you.

The Class-&-Object symbol reflects Objects which the system keeps information about, interacts with, or both. For external systems or devices, this means that such a symbol is an abstraction of that real-world external system.or device—not the external system or device itself.

To depict the system boundaries and external interfaces, and make plain that the OOA symbols are abstractions of the system's responsibilities for the actual person, external system, or device, one may place icons alongside respective OOA Class-&-Object symbols.

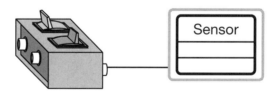

Figure 3.9: An actual sensor and the system's responsibilities for a sensor

Such icons apply only when an interface to an other system or device is involved; the icons are optional, and may be used to improve overall model understandability.

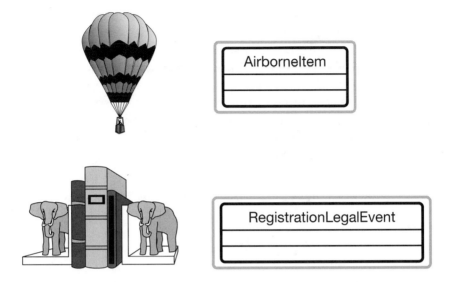

Figure 3.10: Thing or event remembered

Things or events remembered. Next, consider the problem domain for an event remembered. Is there a point in time or an historical event that must be observed and recorded by the system? For example, a motor vehicle registration system must remember the point in time when someone gets a title for a motor vehicle; it's a legal event, and certain data must be captured by statute, e.g., the type of ownership evidence presented. On the other hand, if a system monitors a nuclear reactor, and an incident occurs, then information must be kept about that historical event, over time: who, what, when, where, how, why.

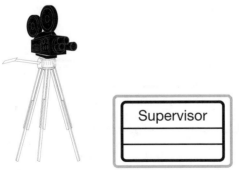

Figure 3.11: Role played

Roles played. What role or roles do human beings play in the system under study? Class-&-Objects representing people occur in two types: those representing users of the system (e.g., a clerk who interacts with the system), and those representing people who do not interact directly with the system, but about whom information is kept by the system (e.g., a motor vehicle owner). Supervisors and Clerks are both reasonably human, yet they may play different roles in the system; subsequent investigation of Attributes and Services will capture the distinction in detail.

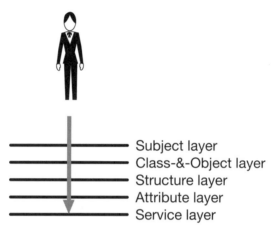

Subject layer
Class-&-Object layer
Structure layer
Attribute layer
Service layer

Figure 3.12: Depicting human interaction: a preferred approach

Yet what about human interaction? Such interaction runs across nearly all of an OOA model. In fact, the human(s) can be thought of as interacting with the entire model, invoking Services as desired—e.g., create, connect, access, release—provided, of course, that any corresponding Service preconditions are satisfied. And this is our preference in OOA modeling.

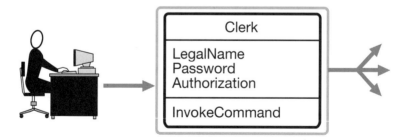

Figure 3.13: Depicting human interaction: an alternative

However, if one wants to show this interaction on the OOA model itself, it can be done as shown. With an icon representing a person, one can also add a description of the operational concepts (also known as the task flow or work flow) for a person playing that role.

Note the multi-headed Message Connection arrow. This notation should be used only when the graphical inclusion of all of the corresponding Message Connections would make the model unreadable.

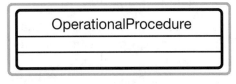

Figure 3.14: Operational procedure

Operational procedures. What operational procedure does the system have to hold over time, to guide human-computer interaction? This kind of Class-&-Object comes up when the system's responsibilities includes needed remembrance of particular operational or work-flow steps which (1) are sequences not inherent in the problem domain constraints, but (2) are within the system's responsibilities to hold over time. Attributes might include operational procedure name, required authorization level, and a description of the steps in the procedure.

Figure 3.15: Site

Sites. What physical location, office, or site does the system under consideration need knowledge of? For example, consider an embedded system that will be set up and configured at a particular latitude, longitude, altitude, and terrain profile. A site Class-&-Object may represent one or many sites; it depends upon the problem domain under consideration.

Figure 3.16: Organizational unit

Organizational units. What organizational units do the humans belong to? For example, a motor vehicle clerk works within a county organization—so "County" should be considered as a potential Class-&-Object. And if the system needs to keep track of information about a county (e.g., manager name, address, fee percentages, and the like) or provide processing pertinent to a county (e.g., determine how much money was collected today), then such a Class-&-Object is needed.

In conclusion, look for structures, other systems, devices, things or events remembered, roles played, operational procedures, sites, and organizational units.

Once you find a candidate Class-&-Object, examine it in light of "What to Consider and Challenge."

3.3.4 What to Consider and Challenge

You've found a candidate Class-&-Object. Perhaps you've found one called "Vehicle." Should you include it as a Class-&-Object in your model?

Consider and challenge potential Class-&-Objects with the following criteria:

- needed remembrance
- needed behavior
- (usually) multiple Attributes
- (usually) more than one Object in a Class
- always-applicable Attributes
- always-applicable Services
- domain-based requirements
- not merely derived results

Think about these things when determining whether or not to include a Class-&-Object in a model, and again when reviewing a model.

Figure 3.17: Needed remembrance

Needed remembrance. Does the system need to remember anything about the Objects in the Class? Look at the problem domain, then the system's responsibilities. Can an Object in the Class be described? What are some of the potential Attributes (capturing its state)? For example, potential Attributes for a clerk include name, password, and authorization. Is knowledge about that real world person of interest to the system under consideration? Is there something about that person that the system needs to remember? If not, the validity and relevance of a corresponding Class-&-Object symbol is suspect—remember, many Class-&-Objects in the real world may be interesting, and may come up in discussions with the clients, but they may not turn out to be relevant to the system under consideration.

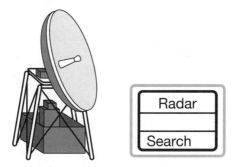

Figure 3.18: Needed behavior

Needed behavior. Does an Object need to provide some behavior (processing)? As long as needed remembrance applies, then Services will be needed—at the very least to create, connect, access, and release an Object.

Conceivably an Object could have required Services, but no required remembrance (Attributes). For example, an external system Class-&-Object, with just one Object in the Class, could conceivably have only Services (and no Attributes) for dealing with the corresponding system interface. In practice, this has yet to occur. The one time the authors observed Class-&-Object symbols with only Services inside, the analyst had been trying to use OOA notation with DFD-style functional thinking; this does not lead to effective OOA results.

Figure 3.19: (Usually) multiple Attributes

(Usually) multiple Attributes. This criterion helps filter out potential Class-&-Objects when an analyst gets to a level that is too low in his thinking. If an Object (e.g., "InstalledSite") has just one Attribute (e.g., "Address"), get suspicious; it's likely that "Address" may be better included as an Attribute, which may appear in a number of Class-&-Objects, rather than as an individual Object in its own right. The key is the leveling of detail: Class-&-Objects are further described by Attributes, which are then further described in a Class-&-Object specification.[5]

(Usually) more than one Object in a Class. Next, challenge Classes with just one Object. Class-&-Object symbols labeled "this vehicle" and "that vehicle" are suspect.

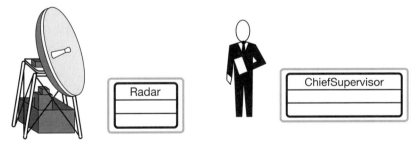

Figure 3.20: (Usually) more than one Object in a Class

[5] This is examined in more detail in Chapter 6.

Yet if a Class with just a single Object really does reflect the problem domain, so be it. For example, an air traffic control system might have a "Radar" Object, with only one radar in the problem domain.

Or there might be a "ChiefSupervisor" Class-&-Object at the root of a Whole-Part. But if another Class-&-Object with the *same* Attributes and Services exists, and if it accurately reflects the reality of the problem domain, then consider using just one Class-&-Object instead. And, if another Object with *similar* Attributes and similar Services exists, and it depicts the real world, then consider using a Generalization-Specialization Structure, as described in Chapter 4.

Figure 3.21: Always-applicable Attributes

Always-applicable Attributes.   Can you identify a set of Attributes that apply to each Object in the Class? Every time a system knows about the occurrence of an Object, it should have a value for each Attribute. For example, a "Building" Class-&-Object in a real estate listing system might include location, price, list date, and size. Yet what about number of bedrooms and number of bathrooms? These Attributes may apply only to certain kinds of buildings. If this is the case, it's an indication that a Generalization-Specialization Structure could be developed here; we'll discuss this in more detail in Chapter 4.

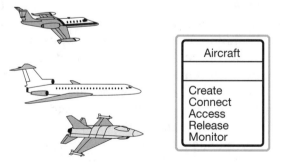

Figure 3.22: Always-applicable Services

Always-applicable Services. Can you identify always-applicable Services—i.e., behavior (processing) that applies to each Object in a Class? Services may be algorithmically simple (create, connect, access, release) or algorithmically complex (calculate, initialize/monitor/terminate). If the Services are the same for each Object in the Class, that's fine; however, if the Services vary for different Objects, that variation is an indication that a Gen-Spec Structure could be added.

This discussion indicates that you should consider always-applicable Attributes and Services in a general sense while investigating the problem domain for an initial set of Class-&-Objects. Then, as you consider the Attributes and Services in greater detail, you'll discover finer detail and nuances that you can bring into the model as well.

Domain-based requirements. Domain-based requirements are those requirements the system *must* have, regardless of the computer technology used to build (design and implement) the system. When radars and sensors (for example, a device that measures temperature, pressure, or power) are in the problem domain, then regardless of the computer technology that will eventually be employed, we should expect to see corresponding "Radar" and "Sensor" Class-&-Object symbols. But computer system architectures (centralized, distributed, or replicated), disk drives, display terminals, batching up of computational results for faster perceived performance, time vs. size trade-offs, and the like are design and implementation considerations. The choice of one or two computers is a design decision, regardless of when that decision happens to be made chronologically during system development; so is the packing and shipping, and receiving and routing, of requests and updates between machines.

Whether the project chooses to use a hand-held display device, a lap-top, a sophisticated graphics system, or a large screen display is a design selection; as an analyst, focus first on determining what information and behavior are required of the system. Use prototypes and operational concept studies to define and refine what the required information content is all about. But particular screen sequences, menus, windows, and the like belong in a design folder, and ultimately in the design; they are mechanisms for implementing the description of the system's responsibilities.

Similarly, task management and data management ideas belong in a design folder, and ultimately in the design.

Keep a file of design notes. It helps keep frustration down. And it helps people avoid premature design decisions or biases. Several months later, a design idea may not appear quite so appealing. And either way, the systems analysis and specification are not burdened with particular implementation details. They remain focused as abstractions, emphasizing the problem domain and its Class-&-Objects, Structures, Attributes, and Services.

It is fair game for an analyst to impose design constraints. For example, if a particular algorithm *must* be used—e.g., because of stringent constraints on the result, or because of some legal statute—make it a requirement. Otherwise, specify the accuracy of the determined value, and allow the designer to select the algorithm appropriate in the context of the available computing resources.

The design team will add Class-&-Objects to provide design-dependent processing—human interaction, task management (including external interface protocols), and data management.

Even if a particular hardware/software architecture is mandated by the client or by some external statute, and will never, ever change, keep it out of the systems analysis, organization, and specification. Why? First, to keep the analysis and specification abstractions as simple as possible. Second, to avoid massive re-work when the never-ever-changeable does indeed change. Then the requirements can be mapped to different architectures as needed, to assess timing and sizing implications.

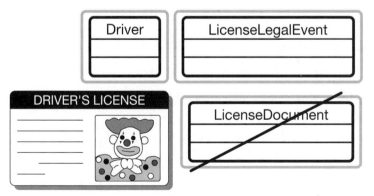

Figure 3.23: Not merely derived results

Not merely derived results. Finally, avoid merely derived results—e.g., "client's age" in a system that already remembers the client's date of birth. In a model of domain-based requirements, derived results muddy the picture. Gathering interim calculation results is a design decision; the requirement is most succinctly stated as the ability to do a calculation as if from scratch each time. Eventually the design team can add derived Class-&-Objects (and add the Services governing immediate, periodic, or on-demand calculation) for performance considerations. For example, consider a problem domain with actual drivers' licenses, along with many other printed reports. Avoid making each printed report a Class-&-Object; such reports are somewhat arbitrary packages of domain-based and non-domain-based data. You may want to consider the content of existing reports, to see what Class-&-Objects the data might describe. For example, while observing an actual driver's license, one might consider (1) roles played (Driver), (2) events remembered (License LegalEvent, for the legal event itself, and, if each issuance needs to be remembered, DocumentIssuanceEvent), and (3) things remembered (if the physical pieces of paper need to be inventoried and tracked, LicenseDocument).

So, avoid derived results as Class-&-Objects; instead, capture the Attributes and Services in Class-&-Objects from which such derived results can be obtained.

In conclusion, consider and challenge needed remembrance, needed behavior, (usually) multiple Attributes, (usually) more than one Object in a Class, always-applicable Attributes, always-applicable Services, domain-based requirements, and not merely derived results.

3.4 CLASS-&-OBJECTS—KEY POINTS

Summarizing the "Finding Class-&-Objects" activity:

NOTATION—Finding Class-&-Objects

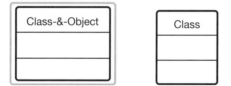

Figure 3.24: Class-&-Object notation and Class notation

STRATEGY—Finding Class-&-Objects

Object. An abstraction of something in a problem domain, reflecting the capabilities of a system to keep information about or interact with it; an encapsulation of Attribute values and their exclusive Services.

Class. A collection of Objects which can be described with the same Attributes and Services.

Class-&-Object. A term meaning *"a Class and the Objects in that Class."*

How to name

Singular noun or adjective & noun; describe a single Object in the Class; standard vocabulary for the problem domain.

Where to look

Observe first-hand; listen actively; check previous OOA results; other systems; read, read, read; and prototype.

What to look for

Look for structures, other systems, devices, things or events remembered, roles played, operational procedures, sites, and organizational units.

What to consider and challenge

Needed remembrance, needed behavior, (usually) multiple Attributes, (usually) more than one Object in a Class, always-applicable Attributes, always-applicable Services, domain-based requirements, and not merely derived results.

EXAMPLE—Sensor System

The example system monitors sensors and critical sensors; it also reports problem conditions.

Problem Statement. Each sensor is described by its model (manufacturer and model number), initialization sequence (sent to the sensor to initialize it), conversion (scale factor, bias, and unit of measure), sampling interval, location, state (on, off, or standby), current value, and alarm threshold.

In addition, critical sensors are described by tolerance (the tolerance of the sampling interval).

The system reports an alarm whenever a sensor threshold is met or exceeded.

Observations. Potential Class-&-Objects include two devices (Sensor, CriticalSensor), a thing/event remembered (AlarmEvent), and a role played (Clerk). Yet for this example, the system's responsibilities are going to be quite constrained: suppose that the client wants to *omit* both alarm event remembrance (i.e., alarm history) and roles played (i.e., accountability or access control).

So the model consists of Sensor and CriticalSensor. Additional details will follow with subsequent OOA activities and layers.

Figure 3.25: Sensor System—Class-&-Object layer

EXAMPLE—Registration and Title System

The registration and title example comes from practice, applying object-oriented approaches during the development of a motor vehicle registration and title system.[6]

Problem Statement. The registration and title system maintains information on the following:

---

[6] The details for such a system would be somewhat different in various states, provinces, and countries.

Organization—name, manager, address, telephone

Clerk—legal name, address, user name, authorization, begin date, end date

Owner—legal name, address, telephone

Title—number, ownership evidence, surrendered title, title date & time, fee

Registration—date & time, date and time start, date and time end, plate [issuer, year, type, number], sticker [year, type, number], fee

Vehicle—number, year, make, model, body style, color, cost; plus

> for trucks: number of passengers, mileage, powered by, temporary gross weight
>
> for motorcycle: number of passengers, mileage
>
> for trailers: gross weight
>
> for travel trailer: number of passengers, mileage, powered by, body number, length

Clerks are accountable for registrations and titles issued (plus the fees accepted).

Each Clerk belongs to an organization (county, region, or headquarters).

The system issues registration renewal notices.

Observations. The potential Class-&-Objects include another system (Vehicle), events remembered (Legal Event, specializing into TitleLegalEvent and RegistrationLegalEvent), roles played (Person, specializing into OwnerPerson, ClerkPerson, ClerkOwnerPerson), and an organization (Organization, anticipating that each organization can be described with the same Attributes and Services; otherwise, separate County, Region, and Headquarters Class-&-Object symbols would apply here). Additional details will follow with subsequent OOA activities and layers.

The notational difference between Class-&-Object and its variation (called a Class) is discussed in the next chapter.

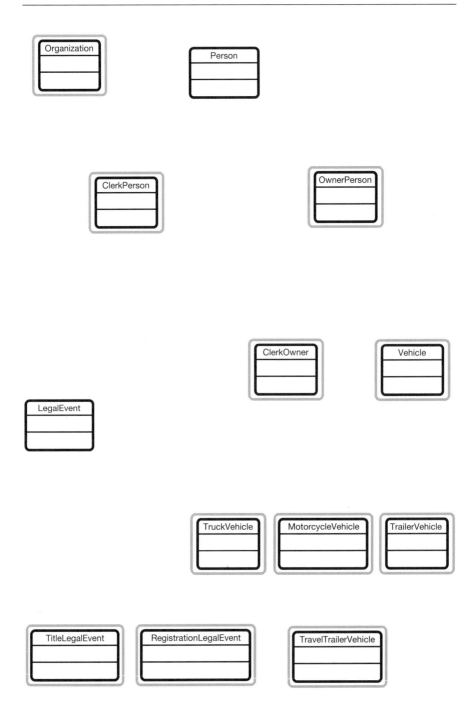

Figure 3.26: Registration and Title System—Class-&-Object layer

EXAMPLE—Real-Time Airlift System

Another example is derived from a recently developed airlift system.

Problem Statement. The Real-Time Airlift System (RTAS) provides automated support for mission planners and airlift personnel.

First, consider those things which concern mission planners. Shipment items include both passengers (name, rank, number, origin, now located at, destination) and cargo items (weight, dimensions, description, number, origin, now located at, destination). Flight segments (number, origin, destination) consist of some number of shipment items. Missions (code name, number, description) consist of some number of flight segments.

Airlift personnel assign aircraft (call number, status, model, capacity, location) for each flight segment and keep track of which shipment items are actually loaded into a corresponding aircraft; they plan around aircraft failure (failure date and time, description, corrective action).

Aircraft locations may be entered manually, or determined by the following processing:

- Radar is commanded to search the airspace (radar parameters include frequency, pulse interval, location, search space); it will find airborne items (with date, time, and position).
- Trajectories (confidence level) are built, and future position can be predicted.
- A trajectory and a known aircraft may be mapped, one to another.

RTAS is constrained to detect and report an airborne item within 550 ms. RTAS shall update and report the corresponding trajectory (and matched aircraft, if any) within a subsequent 1100 ms.

Observations. Initial Class-&-Objects include other systems (Aircraft, Radar), events remembered (Failure, possibly different kinds of failures, AircraftFailure, and possibly different kinds of aircraft failures), things remembered (Mission, FlightSegment, and Shipment Item, specializing into PassengerShipmentItem and CargoShipmentItem), and roles played (MissionPlanner, Airlift-Person, and, again, PassengerShipmentItem).

Yet in this example, suppose that the client only wants to keep track of aircraft failures, not others. Moreover, the client does not want to control access or keep accountability information on

MissionPlanner or AirliftPerson. The result is shown in the accompanying Class-&-Object layer. Additional details will follow with subsequent OOA activities and layers.

Also, note that this system does have real-time performance constraints. In practice, real-time constraints and critical threads of execution often affect *only a portion* of the overall OOA model. Such real-time constraints and the critical threads of execution will be addressed in Chapter 7.

The notational difference between Class-&-Object and its variation (called a Class) is discussed in the next chapter.

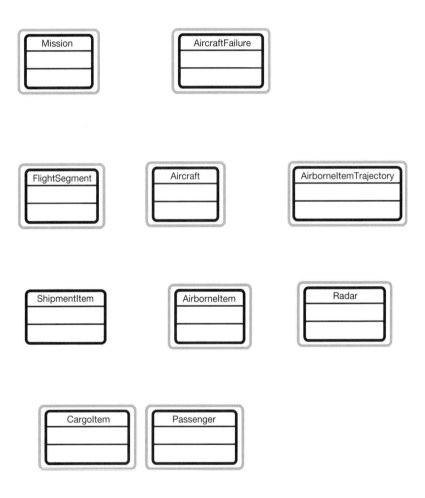

Figure 3.27: Real-Time Airlift System—Class-&-Object layer

4

Identifying Structures

This chapter examines Generalization-Specialization (Gen-Spec) and Whole-Part Structures—what, why, how, and key points.

4.1 STRUCTURES—WHAT

Webster's defines "structure" with the following:

> Structure. A manner of organization.
> [Webster's, 1977]

In OOA, the term "Structure" is defined reflecting both the problem domain and the system's responsibilities:

> Structure. Structure is an expression of problem-domain complexity, pertinent to the system's responsibilities. The term "Structure" is used as an overall term, describing both Generalization-Specialization (Gen-Spec) Structure[1] and Whole-Part Structure.[2]

Generalization-Specialization (Gen-Spec) Structure may be viewed as part of the "distinguishing between Classes" aspect of the three basic methods of organization that pervade all human thinking. An example is the generalization Vehicle, and the specialization TruckVehicle. Less formally, a Gen-Spec Structure—from the specialization's perspective—can be thought of as an "is a" or "is a kind of" Structure, e.g., a TruckVehicle is a (is a kind of) Vehicle. Within Gen-Spec Structures, inheritance applies, with an explicit representation of more general Attributes and Services followed by pertinent specializations.

[1] Generalization-Specialization (Gen-Spec) Structure" replaces an earlier term, "Classification Structure." While the older term is acceptable and consistent with the classification schemes used in bibliographic cataloging, the actual Structure being depicted is more specifically one of Generalization-Specialization.

[2] "Whole-Part Structure" replaces an earlier term, "Assembly Structure." While "Assembly Structure" is acceptable, it presents language translation problems (often meaning something solely mechanical in nature). "Whole-Part" provides a better all-inclusive term, covering the variety of such Structures presented in this chapter.

Whole-Part Structure is one of the three basic methods of organization that pervade all human thinking. An example is the whole Vehicle, and the part Engine. Less formally, a Whole-Part Structure—from the whole's perspective—can be thought of as a "has a" Structure, e.g., a Vehicle has an Engine.

4.2 STRUCTURES—WHY

Gen-Spec and Whole-Part Structures focus the attention of the analyst and problem domain experts on the complexity of multiple Class-&-Objects.

Moreover, in using Structures, analysts push the edges of the system's responsibilities within a domain, uncovering additional Class-&-Objects (e.g., implicit in a "requesting document") that might otherwise be missed.

In addition, for Gen-Spec Structure in particular, inheritance applies, so that generalized Attributes and Services are identified and specified once, then specialized appropriately.

4.3 STRUCTURES—HOW

For each Class-&-Object, examine each Class for Gen-Spec Structure, and each Object for Whole-Part Structure.

4.3.1 Gen-Spec Structure—How

Here we present notation and strategy, and then Gen-Spec Structure hierarchies and lattices.

4.3.1.1 Gen-Spec Structure Notation

Gen-Spec Structure is shown with a Generalization Class at the top and Specialization Classes below, with lines drawn between them. A semi-circle marking distinguishes Classes as forming a Gen-Spec Structure.

The notation is directional—it uses a line drawn outward from the semicircle midpoint to "point" to the generalization—so

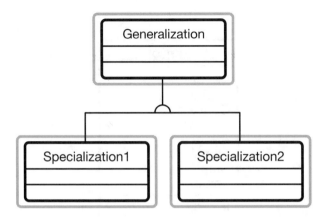

Figure 4.1: Gen-Spec Structure notation

a Structure could be drawn at any angle; however, consistently placing the generalization higher and the specializations lower produces an easier-to-understand model.

The endpoints of a Gen-Spec Structure line are positioned to reflect a mapping between Classes (rather than between Objects).

Each specialization is named in such a way that it can stand on its own. An appropriate name for the specialization will typically be the name(s) of its corresponding generalization(s), accompanied by a qualifying name which describes the nature of the specialization. For example, for a generalization called Sensor, specializations "Critical-Sensor" and "StandardSensor" are preferred over just merely "Critical" or "Standard."

Class-&-Object symbols appear for all bottom-most specializations. At other places, either Class-&-Object or Class symbols may be appropriate. Consider the following examples.

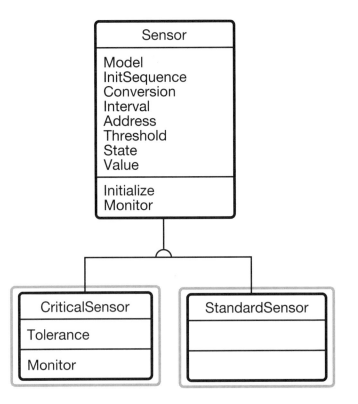

Figure 4.2: Using a Class as a generalization

Here, an actual sensor is either a critical sensor or a standard sensor. "Sensor" is a Class without any *directly* corresponding Objects; instead, the corresponding Objects are reflected in those of its specializations which are Class-&-Objects.

Since no added Attributes and no added or extended Services apply to standard sensors, this particular Structure may be further refined into the following:

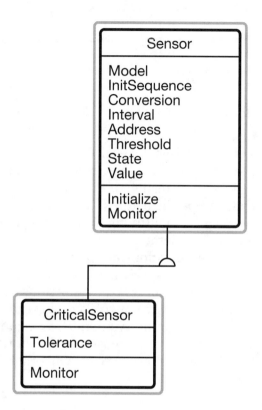

Figure 4.3: Using a Class-&-Object as a generalization

Here, an actual sensor is either a critical sensor or just a sensor. So, again, in Gen-Spec notation, Class-&-Object symbols appear for all bottom-most specializations; at other places, either Class-&-Object or Class symbols may be appropriate. (Additional examples are shown throughout this chapter.)

4.3.1.2 Gen-Spec Structure Strategy

Consider each Class as a generalization. For its potential specializations, ask:

- Is it in the problem domain?
- Is it within the system's responsibilities?
- Will there be inheritance?
- Will the specializations meet the "what to consider and challenge" criteria for Class-&-Objects (as presented in chapter 3)?

In a similar fashion, consider each Class as a specialization. For its potential generalizations, ask these same questions.

Check previous OOA results in the same and similar problem domains. Which Gen-Spec Structures can be directly reused? What lessons can be learned for identifying Gen-Spec Structures pertinent to the system under consideration?

Also, if many specializations are possible, it's very helpful to first consider the simplest specialization and the most elaborate specialization, and then to follow with the various ones in between. For example, there may be dozens of specializations of a "store" (something placed under a military aircraft). By examining the simplest store (a dumb bomb) and the most complex store (an advanced missile), one establishes a pattern by which all other specializations can be developed.

Aircraft

JetPlaneAircraft   HelicopterAircraft

Figure 4.4: Identifying a Gen-Spec Structure

For example, consider the Class "Aircraft" as a generalization. It could be specialized in a variety of ways:

- JetPlaneAircraft and HelicopterAircraft
- CivilianAircraft and MilitaryAircraft
- JetAircraft and PropellerAircraft
- FixedWingAircraft and MovableWingAircraft
- CommercialAircraft and PrivateAircraft

Let's consider the potential specialization of jet aircraft and propeller aircraft.

- Do the specializations JetPlaneAircraft and HelicopterAircraft "make sense" as specializations within the problem domain at hand? If the distinction is not in the problem domain, then the specializations are not needed.

- Does the system need to recognize the difference between a JetPlaneAircraft and a HelicopterAircraft? How are the system's responsibilities for these specializations different? If no difference exists, then the specializations are not needed.

- Will there be inheritance—meaning that some Attributes and Services apply to all Aircraft, and then specialize into Attributes and Services that apply just to JetPlaneAircraft, and others that apply just to HelicopterAircraft?

- Will the specializations meet the "what to consider and challenge" criteria for Class-&-Objects (as presented in chapter 3)? For this example, let's consider some variations on what we might see at this point:

   If the *only* distinction between JetPlaneAircraft and Helicopter-Aircraft is the aircraft type, then use Aircraft with an Attribute (e.g., Type) with an enumeration of values (e.g., JetPlane or Helicopter). No Gen-Spec Structure is needed here.

   If the *only* distinction between the specializations is that the system is responsible for knowing a jet plane aircraft's maximum thrust (but not responsible for knowing this for a helicopter), then use Aircraft with an Attribute (e.g., MaxThrust) with values. No Gen-Spec Structure is needed here.

   If a Specialization Class adds no Attributes or Services, it is not needed—unless it portrays a Class with multiple direct generalizations (portrayed in a Gen-Spec lattice; an example of this is included later in this chapter).

For each Class, we can also consider it as a specialization, and consider its potential generalizations. Aircraft is a specialization of Transport. And so the same questions must be asked:

- Is it in the problem domain?
- Is it within the system's responsibilities?
- Will there be inheritance?
- Will the specializations meet the "what to consider and challenge" criteria for Class-&-Objects (as presented in chapter 3)?

One of the criteria for a Gen-Spec Structure is whether or not it reflects a generalization-specialization in the problem domain. Do not introduce a Gen-Spec Structure just for the sake of extracting out a common Attribute.

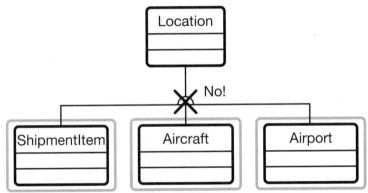

Figure 4.5: An inappropriate Gen-Spec Structure

Note that in this example, the Class names themselves do not portray generalization, then specialization. Modeling understandability takes precedence over factoring out common (or seemingly common) Attributes.

4.3.1.3 Gen-Spec Structure: Hierarchy and Lattice

Each Gen-Spec Structure forms either a hierarchy or a lattice.[3,4]

[3] These alternatives are referred to in programming languages as single inheritance and multiple inheritance, respectively. For OOA, both hierarchy and lattice shapes are of interest, being useful in effective analysis modeling. We leave the "favorite language" debates and religious fervor to language zealots.

[4] Previously, we used an "override" notation, in order to extract some of the redundancy that may come up in a hierarchy. With the addition of lattices, that notation is no longer needed; such "overriding" would indicate that something (a specialization, Attribute, or Service) is placed incorrectly within a Gen-Spec Structure (below a generalization it does not belong under).

In practice, the most common form of Gen-Spec Structure is a hierarchy.

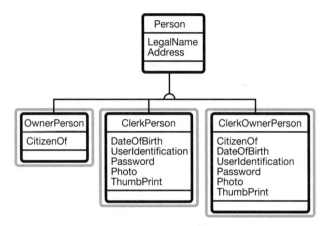

Figure 4.6: Person Gen-Spec Structure, as a hierarchy

In this example, a person is an owner, a clerk, or a clerk and owner. Yet with some hierarchies, such as this one, certain redundancies appear across the specializations.

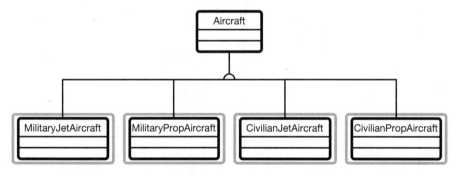

Figure 4.7: Aircraft Gen-Spec Structure, as a hierarchy

In this example, an aircraft is a military jet aircraft, a military prop aircraft, a civilian jet aircraft, or a civilian prop aircraft. Yet the hierarchy fails to capture any commonality across military aircraft, civilian aircraft, jet aircraft, or prop aircraft. So with some hierarchies, such as this one, certain redundancies appear across the specializations.

With a Gen-Spec lattice, some additional problem-domain specializations can be brought to light; moreover, more Attribute and Service commonality can be explicitly represented.

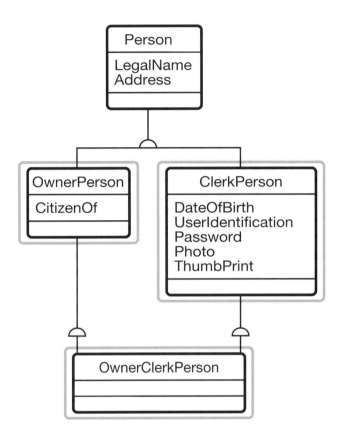

Figure 4.8: Person Gen-Spec Structure, as a lattice

This example shows that the problem domain has persons in it, and that any given person in the domain is an owner, a clerk, or both. The OwnerClerkPerson specialization portrays a Class with multiple direct generalizations; it indicates that an Object can exist which inherits a combination of the Attributes and Services from its ancestors. Moreover, if additional Attributes and Services applied to an owner-clerk, they would appear in the OwnerClerkPerson specialization.

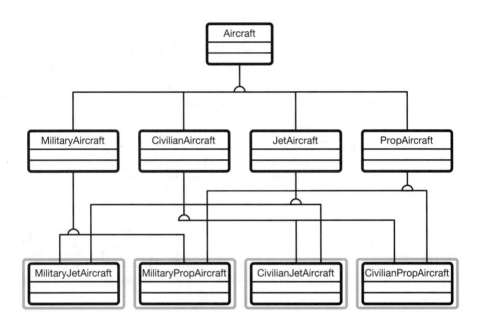

Figure 4.9: Aircraft Gen-Spec Structure, as a lattice

The lattice:

- Highlights additional specializations
- Explicitly captures commonality
- Only modestly increases model complexity

Observe that the lattice structure could become unwieldy with more and more specializations. This has not come up in practice. If this should occur, however, consider reorganizing part of the lattice into a hierarchy; this may be more effective in communicating the problem domain and the system's responsibilities.

Using the same Attribute or Service name in more than one immediate generalization leads to problems during Class-&-Object specification. For example, if the Service "CalculatePayloadWeight" applies to both MilitaryAircraft and JetAircraft, then what is inherited by MilitaryJetAircraft is unclear. Avoid such naming conflicts within a lattice; this is a simple solution. Otherwise, the MilitaryJet-Aircraft "Class-&-Object" symbol must include the conflicting service name, and the corresponding specification must resolve what the required behavior is for a MilitaryJetAircraft.

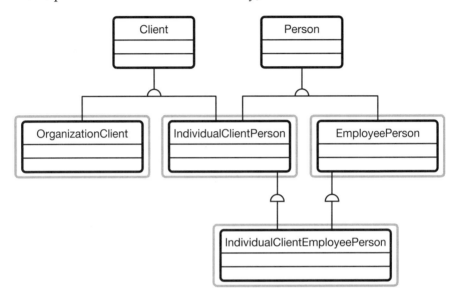

Figure 4.10: Client and Person Gen-Spec Structure lattice

This Gen-Spec Structure lattice captures an overlap between two different Gen-Spec Structures, one for Client and one for Person. A client is an organization client (e.g., a corporation, a trust, a propriety) or an individual client person. A person is an individual client person, an employee person, or both. So an actual Object is one of the following: an organization client, an individual client, an employee, or both an individual client and an employee.

More often in practice, multiple Gen-Spec Structures appear side-by-side, and are mapped to one another with Instance Connections (discussed in Chapter 6).

4.3.2 Whole-Part Structure—How

Whole-part is one of the basic methods of organization that pervade all human thinking. In problem domain investigation, it proves very helpful in identifying Class-&-Objects at the edges of a problem domain, and at the edges of the system's responsibilities in that domain. It also groups together Class-&-Objects based upon this special whole-part meaning.

Here we present notation and strategy, including the different kinds of Whole-Part Structures.

4.3.2.1 Whole-Part Structure Notation

Whole-Part Structure is shown with a whole Object (of a Class-&-Object symbol) at the top, and then a part Object (of a Class-&-Object symbol) below, with a line drawn between them. A triangle marking distinguishes Objects as forming a Whole-Part Structure.

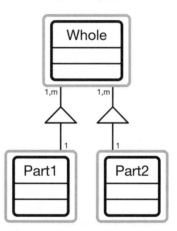

Figure 4.11: Whole-Part Structure notation

The notation is directional, so that the Structure could be drawn at any angle; however, consistently placing the whole higher and the parts lower produces an easier-to-understand model. This is deliberate: we want to portray the fact that a whole has some number of parts. Also, note that a whole may have different kinds of parts.

The endpoints of a Whole-Part Structure line are positioned to reflect a mapping between Objects (rather than between Classes).

Each end of a Whole-Part Structure line is marked with an amount or range, indicating the number of parts that a whole may have, and vice versa, *at any given moment in time.*

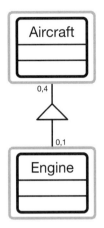

Figure 4.12: Whole-Part Structure example

In this example, an aircraft is an assembly of

- possibly no engines (a glider!),
- at most four engines

  and an engine is part of

- possibly no aircraft,
- at most one aircraft

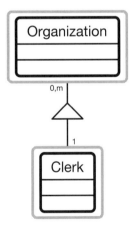

Figure 4.13: Another Whole-Part Structure example

In this example, an organization is a collection of

- possibly no clerks,
- at most many clerks

and a clerk is member of

- exactly one organization

If the mappings to another Object *over time* are to be remembered, then that other Object needs a DateTime or Status Attribute, to distinguish the most recent or active Object (respectively) from the others.

4.3.2.2 Whole-Part Structure Strategy

The strategy consists of what to look for, followed by what to consider or challenge.

Investigating whole-part may point out the need for a Class-&-Object, perhaps one not even mentioned in the "requesting document" from the client. When asked about the new Class-&-Object, a client may say:

1. "That's none of your concern. I've got another system to do that."
2. "Of course you must know about pilots. That's implicit in the documentation I gave you."
3. "That's a good point. What's the impact on the project budget and schedule if we include this in the model?"

In this fashion, analysts use Whole-Part Structures to push the edges of a problem domain and a system's responsibilities.

What to Look For

When looking for potential Whole-Part Structures, consider these variations:

- Assembly-Parts
- Container-Contents
- Collection-Members (and its different varieties)

In addition, check previous OOA results in the same and similar problem domains. Which Whole-Part Structures can be directly re-used? What lessons can be learned for identifying Whole-Part Structures pertinent to the system under consideration?

Now let's consider some examples of these variations of Whole-Part Structure.

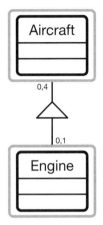

Figure 4.14: Whole-Part Structure—assembly-parts

An aircraft is an assembly, with engine(s) as parts. Such an assembly physically exists, and is readily observed (we can go out and kick one).

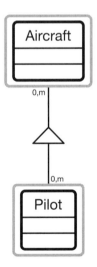

Figure 4.15: Whole-Part Structure—container-contents

Here, the aircraft is considered as a container. Pilots are inside. And if the problem domain and system's responsibilities include knowing about and assigning qualified pilot(s) to specific aircraft, then a Pilot Class-&-Object is needed.

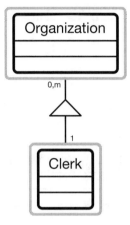

Figure 4.16: Whole-Part Structure—collection-members

An organization is a collection of clerks.

Another example of collection-members is a FlightPlan as an *ordered* collection of FlightSegment members:

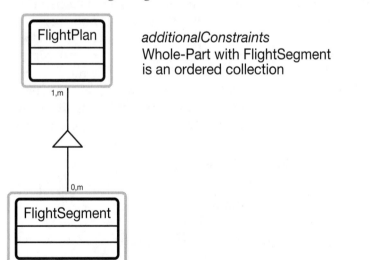

Figure 4.17: Whole-Part Structure—collection-members (with a constraint)

The "ordered" constraint may be specified in the Class-&-Object specification of the whole (in this example, for FlightPlan).

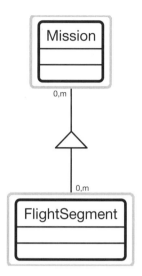

Figure 4.18: Whole-Part Structure—collection-members ("mental model only")

Whole-part is one of the basic methods of organization that pervade all human thinking. Problem domain experts apply collection-member—"mental model only"—to manage complexity of a problem domain. For example, consider Missions consisting of some number of Flight Segments. We can't go out and kick it. We can't observe it. It is a mental model abstraction used in the problem domain. And it can be a useful abstraction, both in pushing the edges of the model and in guiding a reader through a model.

The alternative modeling choice is to use an Instance Connection, discussed in Chapter 6. It's weaker in meaning (it's not one of the basic methods of organization that pervade all human thinking), yet it still captures the mapping.

What to Consider and Challenge

Consider each Object as a whole. For its potential parts, ask:

- Is it in the problem domain?
- Is it within the system's responsibilities?
- Does it capture more than just a status value?
- If not, then just include an Attribute for it within the whole.
- Does it provide a useful abstraction in dealing with the problem domain?

Also, in a similar fashion, consider each Object as a part. For each potential whole, ask these same questions.

Pilot   Engine   CargoItem

Figure 4.19: Identifying a Whole-Part Structure

For example, consider an aircraft. What are its potential parts? Let's examine engines.

- Does an engine make sense in this domain? If the domain is "meal services," probably not. If the domain is "air transportation," then it makes sense. Let's use "air transportation" for this example.

  Yes, in this example it's in the problem domain.

- Is an engine within the system's responsibilities? Does the system need to know about or interact with engines?

  Yes, for "air transportation" it could be part of the system's responsibilities.

- Does an Engine Object capture more than just a status value?

  If the system's responsibilities include only aircraft status (it's working or it's not) or engine status (the aircraft's engines are working or not), then don't use an Engine Class-&-Object; instead, use something like an OperationalStatus Attribute in Aircraft. This captures the system's responsibilities with a simpler model.

  However, if the system's responsibilities for an engine include more than just status—for example, Attributes like Model, SerialNumber, DateOfManufacture, and DateOfOverhaul; or, as another example, a TemperatureWarningThreshold Attribute and a MonitorEngineTemperature Service—then yes, an Engine Class-&-Object is needed.

- Does it provide a useful abstraction in dealing with the problem domain?

  Yes.

Each Object can be considered as a potential part, and also as a potential whole. Thus, suppose Aircraft could be a part of a collection called AirFleet. The same "consider and challenge" questions must be asked.

4.3.3 Multiple Structures

Multiple Structures include various combinations of Gen-Spec Structures, Whole-Part Structures, or both.

Multiple Structures sometimes touch top-to-bottom; otherwise, Instance Connections (part of the Attribute layer, presented in Chapter 6) may map them, side-by-side.

For example:

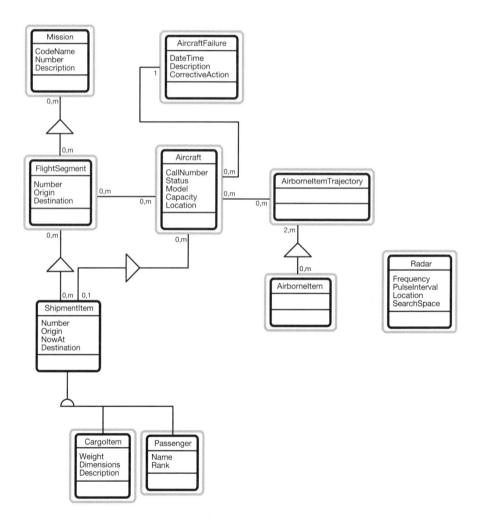

Figure 4.20: Real-Time Airlift System—
Class-&-Object, Structure, and Attribute layers

Certain Structures touch top-to-bottom:

- Mission–FlightSegment Whole-Part and
FlightSegment–ShipmentItem Whole-Part
- FlightSegment–ShipmentItem Whole-Part,
ShipmentItem Gen-Spec, and
Aircraft–ShipmentItem Whole-Part

For other Structures, Instance Connections[5] may map them side-by-side:

- Aircraft–ShipmentItem Whole-Part and
AirborneItemTrajectory–AirborneItem Whole-Part

4.4 STRUCTURES—KEY POINTS

Summarizing the "Identifying Structures" activity:

NOTATION—Identifying Structures

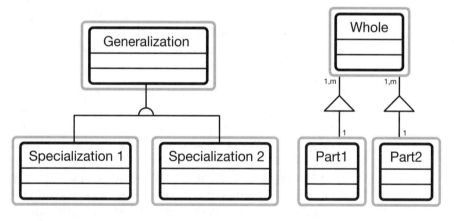

Figure 4.21: Gen-Spec Structure notation and Whole-Part Structure notation

STRATEGY—Identifying Structures

Structure. Structure is an expression of problem-domain complexity, pertinent to the system's responsibilities. The term "Structure" is used as an overall term, describing both Generalization-Specialization (Gen-Spec) and Whole-Part Structures.

---

[5] An Instance Connection is a model of problem domain mapping(s) that one Object needs with other Objects, in order to fulfill its responsibilities. Instance Connections are presented in more detail in Chapter 6.

Gen-Spec Structures

Consider each Class as a generalization. For its potential specializations, ask:

Is it in the problem domain?

Is it within the system's responsibilities?

Will there be inheritance?

Will the specializations meet the "what to consider and challenge" criteria for Class-&-Objects?

Also, in a similar fashion, consider each Class as a specialization. For its potential generalizations, ask these same questions.

Check previous OOA results in the same and similar problem domains.

If many specializations are possible, consider the simplest specialization and the most elaborate specialization, and then follow with the various ones in between.

The most common form of Gen-Spec Structure is a Gen-Spec hierarchy.

Yet a lattice may be used to:

Highlight additional specializations

Explicitly capture commonality

Only modestly increase model complexity

If a lattice structure becomes unwieldy, consider reorganizing part of it into a hierarchy, which may be more effective in communicating the problem domain and the system's responsibilities.

Avoid naming conflicts within a lattice. Otherwise, a specialization which inherits with name conflicts must include the conflicting names, and then resolve what is required in the corresponding specification.

Whole-Part Structures

What to look for:

Consider these variations—

Assembly-Parts

Container-Contents

Collection-Members

Check previous OOA results in the same and similar problem domains.

What to consider and challenge:

Consider each Object as a whole. For its potential parts, ask:

Is it in the problem domain?

Is it within the system's responsibilities?

Does it capture more than just a status value?

If not, then just include a corresponding Attribute within the whole.

Does it provide a useful abstraction in dealing with the problem domain?

Also, in a similar fashion, consider each Object as a part. For each potential whole, ask these same questions.

Multiple Structures

Multiple Structures sometimes touch top-to-bottom; otherwise, Instance Connections may map them, side-by-side.

EXAMPLE—Sensor System

The Sensor System has one Gen-Spec Structure. Each actual sensor for which the system is responsible will be represented as a Sensor Object or a CriticalSensor Object.

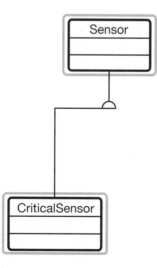

Figure 4.22: Sensor System—Class-&-Object and Structure layers

EXAMPLE—Registration and Title System

The Registration and Title System has three Gen-Spec Structures (Person, LegalEvent, and Vehicle) and one collection-members Whole-Part Structure (Organization–ClerkPerson).

In the Gen-Spec Structures, note the generalizations and the use of either a Class (Person, LegalEvent) or an Class-&-Object (Vehicle). For Person, an Object is actually one of its specializations (Owner-Person, ClerkPerson, ClerkOwnerPerson). For LegalEvent, an Object is also one of its specializations (TitleLegalEvent or Registration-LegalEvent). For Vehicle, an Object may be of the Class Vehicle itself, or one of Vehicle's many specializations.

Also note that certain Structures touch top-to-bottom:

- Organization–ClerkPerson Whole-Part and
  Person Gen-Spec

For other Structures, Instance Connections (part of the Attribute layer) may map them side-by-side:

- Person Gen-Spec and
  LegalEvent Gen-Spec
- LegalEvent Gen-Spec and
  Vehicle Gen-Spec

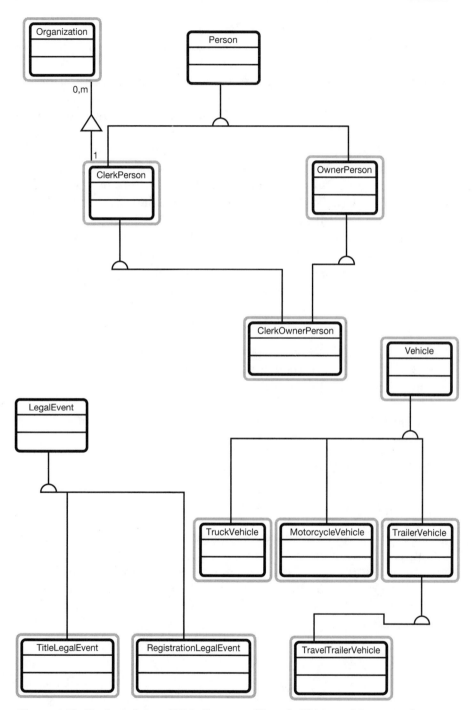

Figure 4.23: Registration and Title System—Class-&-Object and Structure layers

EXAMPLE—Real-Time Airlift System

The Real-Time Airlift System has one Gen-Spec Structure (ShipmentItem), one container-contents Whole-Part Structure (Aircraft-ShipmentItem), one constrained collection-member Whole-Part Structure (AirborneItemTrajectory-AirborneItem), and two collection-member "mental-model-only" Whole-Part Structures (Mission–FlightSegment and FlightSegment–ShipmentItem).

Note that the collection-member "mental-model-only" Whole-Part Structures cannot be kicked or observed; they live only in the minds of problem domain experts. And in this domain, the problem domain experts really do look at a mission as something that consists of some number of flight segments, and any given flight segment as consisting of some number of shipment items. If we failed to get a team consensus on whole-part here, we could model the mappings between the Objects using instance connections; it would be weaker in meaning (it's not one of the basic methods of organization that pervade all human thinking), yet would still capture the mappings.

Certain Structures touch top-to-bottom:

- Mission–FlightSegment Whole-Part and
  FlightSegment–ShipmentItem Whole-Part
- FlightSegment–ShipmentItem Whole-Part,
  ShipmentItem Gen-Spec, and
  Aircraft–ShipmentItem Whole-Part

For other Structures, Instance Connections (part of the Attribute layer) may map them side-by-side:

- Aircraft–ShipmentItem Whole-Part and
  AirborneItemTrajectory Whole-Part

Some Class-&-Objects do not participate in any Structure. For example, consider AircraftFailure. It's not in a Gen-Spec Structure within this domain and the system's responsibilities within it. And it's not in a Whole-Part Structure (it's really a part of an aircraft). We'll see how these additional Class-&-Objects tie in with subsequent OOA activities and layers.

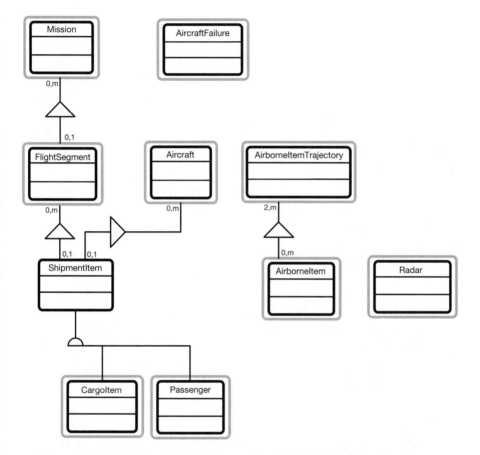

Figure 4.24: Real-Time Airlift System—Class-&-Object and Structure layers

5

Identifying Subjects

This chapter examines Subjects—what, why, how, and key points.

5.1 SUBJECTS—WHAT

Webster's defines "subject" with the following:

> Subject. That which is treated or handled in discussion, study, writing, painting, etc.; a theme, a topic.
> [Webster's, 1977]

In OOA, the term "Subject" is defined reflecting both the problem domain and the system's responsibilities:

> Subject. A Subject is a mechanism for guiding a reader (analyst, problem domain expert, manager, client) through a large, complex model. Subjects are also helpful for organizing work packages on larger projects, based upon initial OOA investigations.

Subjects are strictly a means to an end—they give an overview of a larger OOA model.

The principle behind subjects is an extension of whole-part, called "scale":

> When the proportions of architectural composition are applied to a particular building, the two-termed relationship of the parts to the whole must be harmonized with a third term—the observer. This three-termed relationship is called scale.
> [Britannica, "Architecture, The Art of," 1986]

By incorporating both whole-part and scale principles, Subjects are used to guide a reader through a large model.

The primary basis for identifying Subjects is problem domain complexity, as identified by Gen-Spec Structures and Whole-Part Structures. In this way, Subjects are *parts* used to communicate the *whole* of an overall problem domain and the system's responsibilities.

5.2 SUBJECTS—WHY

The number of Classes in an OOA model is dependent upon the breadth and depth of the problem domain, and the system's responsibilities within it. 35 Classes is average; 110 Classes is large; and for problem domains with several problem sub-domains (e.g., air traffic control), there may be four or five problem sub-domains, with 50–100 Classes in each.

One of the critical success factors for any method and its application is its ability to facilitate communication, avoiding information overload. So for larger models, the question is how to guide the reader into different parts of the model.

Efforts to provide abstractions in the software engineering field have been heavily influenced by George Miller's famous paper, "The magical number seven, plus or minus two: Some limits on our capacity for processing information" [Miller, 1956]. Miller reported that human short-term memory seems to be limited to about 5–9 things at a time (unless a person has been taught to use linked list memory tricks).

Miller added to this work in 1975, with the paper "The magic number seven after fifteen years" [Miller, 1975]. In that paper, Miller reconsidered the matter, showing that, rather than seven plus or minus two, the memory limit is better viewed as three "chunks" of up to three items each.

Miller's results can be interpreted in different ways. One interpretation is that we must *control visibility* to make a system model understandable to the human reader. This control can be accomplished by putting a limit on the number of items shown on a single drawing. Classical structured analysis approaches, such as those popularized in *Structured Analysis and System Specification* [DeMarco, 1978], frequently took this approach. Indeed, certain CASE tools even *enforce* such a guideline. Ugh!

Yet this guideline is a particular interpretation of Miller's research. Its consequence is the need for many diagrams and many *levels* of diagrams. In larger systems, this poses quite a problem—the reader must digest all of the pictorial summaries to understand the textual specifications at the bottom level. This interpretation of Miller's concept controls how much a reader sees at one time—but its drawback is the number of diagrams. For a complex, real-world system, the burden is placed upon the reader to navigate through a hierarchy of diagrams; only the bottom-most ones are described with text.

Another interpretation of Miller's work is the need to *guide reader attention*. This means guiding the reader through a large diagram, using groupings on the diagram to help lead the reader from one area of components to another. This approach is taken in *Structured Systems Analysis: Tools and Techniques* [Gane and Sarson, 1977]. This interpretation means fewer pieces of paper and fewer levels in the hierarchy. For a system modeled with data flow diagrams, this approach might result in a top-level context diagram with just one or two large diagrams below it. The lower diagrams might be as large as a double-size sheet of paper—but parts of the diagram are grouped together to guide the reader's attention to different parts of the model. So, the amount of complexity confronted by the reader *is* controlled, but not with a vertical stack of diagrams.

Effective analysts package information concisely. Miller's work gives us a guideline for such packaging. In OOA, we apply Miller's concept in two ways: control visibility *and* guide reader attention. First, we *control visibility* by controlling the number of layers visible to the analyst or client. The layers can be freely turned on and off at will.[1] For example, the reader may choose to look only at the Class-&-Object and Structure layers, reviewing and refining the model at that level of abstraction. Later, the reader may want to consider just the Class-&-Object and Service layers, examining Message Connection interactions. And so the work can proceed at the level of abstraction one chooses.

We also apply Miller's concept by *guiding reader attention*. OOA adds a Subject layer, which presents the overall model from an even higher perspective. The Subject layer helps a reader review the model, succinctly summarizing the Subjects within the problem domain and the system's responsibilities under consideration.

5.3 SUBJECTS—HOW

This section presents how to select, how to refine, and how to construct.

5.3.1 How to Select

Promote the uppermost Class in each Structure upwards to a Subject. Then promote each Class-&-Object not in a Structure upwards to a Subject.

---

[1] The actual flexibility of "turning on and turning off" layers of the model may be supported by a CASE tool supporting OOA.

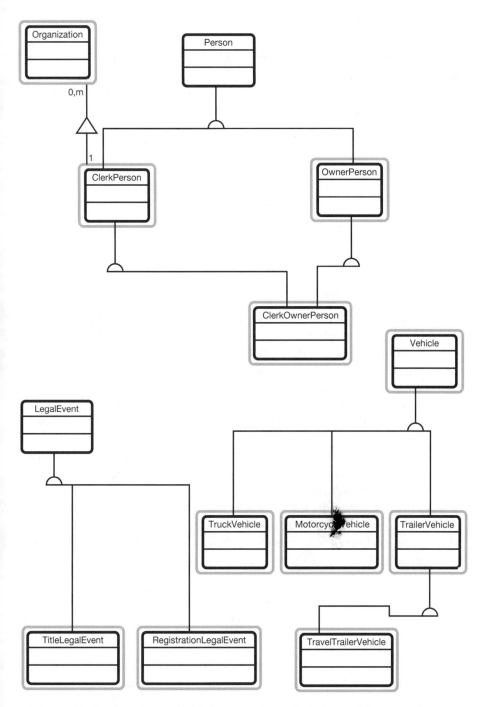

Figure 5.1: Registration and Title System—Class-&-Object and Structure layers

Also, check previous OOA results in the same and similar problem domains. Which Subjects can be directly reused? What lessons can be learned for identifying Subjects pertinent to the system under consideration?

For example, to select Subjects, begin with the Class-&-Object and Structure layers as shown in Figure 5.1. Promote Organization, LegalEvent, Person, and Vehicle upwards to Subjects, as shown in Figure 5.2.

Figure 5.2: Registration and Title System—initial Subjects

5.3.2 How to Refine

To refine this map to guide the reader through a larger model, apply both problem domain and interface complexity considerations.

Refine Subjects by using problem sub-domains. In effect, apply whole-part on the problem domain, in the manner that problem domain experts apply *across the problem domain itself* (e.g., People and Legal), rather than more traditional decomposition of functions (e.g., decomposing the system into Add, Update, Display, and Calculate functions).

Further refine Subjects using minimal interdependencies and minimal interactions between the Subjects. "Interdependencies" are expressed by Structures (discussed in Chapter 4) and Instance Connections (discussed in Chapter 6). "Interactions" are expressed by Message Connections (presented in Chapter 7). Use the Structure, Attribute, and Service layers to guide you in assessing the impact of Subject selection along these lines.

Figure 5.3: Registration and Title System—refining the Subjects

For example, Subjects may be reorganized based upon the problem domain and minimal interdependences, as shown in Figure 5.3.

5.3.3 How to Construct

On the Subject layer, draw each Subject as a simple rectangular box, with a Subject name and number inside. Optionally, list the Classes which are included in the Subject, too.

On other layers, indicate the Subjects with labeled Subject partitioning boxes, to guide the reader from Subject to Subject.

For a large model, consider printing a separate set of diagrams for each Subject, showing connecting Subjects "collapsed" on each set of diagrams, as needed to facilitate communication.

Subjects may be thought of as collapsed, partially expanded (listing their Class-&-Objects), or fully expanded (Subject partitioning boxes, layered along with the other OOA layers); see examples in the "Key Points" section.

A Class-&-Object may be in more than one Subject (when useful in guiding the reader).

Subjects may contain other Subjects, providing a multi-level map to guide a reader through a large model.

OOA applies Miller's "7±2" principle by *controlling visibility* (with layers) and *guiding reader attention* (with Subjects).

5.3.4 When to Add

When should Subjects get introduced into the model? It depends upon the model complexity itself. On very small projects, a Subject layer may not be needed at all (the other layers are simple enough as is).

For projects with about 35 Class-&-Objects, the Subjects can be introduced later in the analysis effort—after the Class-&-Objects are well understood—to guide the various readers through the model.

But larger projects need Subjects right away, to partition the problem domain into problem sub-domains, establish work packages, and move ahead. Here, we recommend that a team of senior analysts do a rapid first-pass identification of Class-&-Objects and Structures, and then identify an initial set of Subjects; such a rapid first pass is sometimes called a "blitz." These Subjects can be assigned to teams. Later, the Subjects can be revisited and fine-tuned, based upon additional understanding of the problem domain and the system's responsibilities within it.

5.4 SUBJECTS—KEY POINTS

Summarizing the "Identifying Subjects" activity:

NOTATION—Identifying Subjects

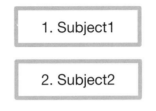

Figure 5.4: Subject notation, collapsed

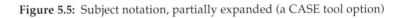

Figure 5.5: Subject notation, partially expanded (a CASE tool option)

Figure 5.6: Subject notation, expanded (when shown with other layers)

STRATEGY—Identifying Subjects

Subject. A Subject is a mechanism for guiding a reader (analyst, problem domain expert, manager, client) through a large, complex model. Subjects are also helpful for organizing work packages on larger projects, based upon initial OOA investigations.

How to select

Promote the uppermost Class in each Structure upwards to a Subject. Then, promote each Class-&-Object not in a Structure upwards to a Subject. Check previous OOA results in the same and similar problem domains.

How to refine

Refine Subjects by using problem sub-domains. Refine Subjects by using minimal interdependencies (Structures, Instance Connections) and minimal interactions (Message Connections) between them; use the Structure, Attribute, and Service layers to guide you.

How to construct

On the Subject layer, draw each Subject as a simple rectangular box, with a Subject name and number inside. Optionally, list the Classes which are included in the Subject, too.

On other layers, indicate the Subjects with labeled Subject partitioning boxes, to guide the reader from Subject to Subject.

For a large model, as needed to facilitate communication, consider using a separate set of layers for each Subject.

Subjects may be thought of as collapsed, partially expanded (listing its Classes-&-Objects), and fully expanded (Subject partitioning boxes, layered on top of other OOA layers).

A Class-&-Object may be in more than one Subject (when useful in guiding the reader).

Subjects may contain other Subjects, providing multi-level map to guide a reader through a large model.

When to Add

Add once an overall map is needed to guide the various readers through the model.

EXAMPLE—Sensor System

The Sensor System model is so small that it has no need for a mechanism for guiding a reader through a larger model. Hence, no Subjects or Subject layer are needed.

```
┌─────────────┐
│  1. Sensor  │
└─────────────┘
```

Figure 5.7: Sensor System—Subject layer (if one is desired for this simple model)

However, if one wanted to include a Subject layer, a single Subject would do just fine.

Example—Registration and Title System

Promote uppermost Classes: Organization, Person, LegalEvent, and Vehicle. Then refine, combining Subjects by problem sub-domains: People, Legal.

Figure 5.8: Registration and Title System—Subject layer

Example—Real-Time Airlift System

Promote uppermost Classes:

- Mission, FlightSegment, ShipmentItem
- Aircraft, AircraftFailure
- AirborneItemTrajectory
- Radar

Refine, combining the Mission–FlightSegment–ShipmentItem multiple Structure:

- Mission
- Aircraft, AircraftFailure
- AirborneItemTrajectory
- Radar

Either refine further, combining:

- by interaction

  Radar

  AirborneItem

  AirborneItemTrajectory

  (these interact; refer to Chapter 7 and the Service layer)
- by interdependency

  Aircraft

  AircraftFailure

  (Aircraft is dependent upon AircraftFailure; refer to Chapter 6 and the Attribute layer)
- resulting in

  Mission

  Positioning

  Aircraft

or refine further, combining by problem sub-domains:

- Mission
- Airlift

  or use both approaches for such additional refining.

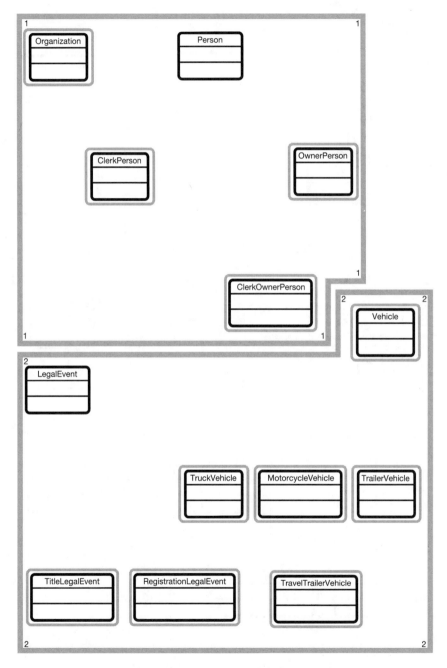

Figure 5.9: Registration and Title System—
Subject and Class-&-Object layers

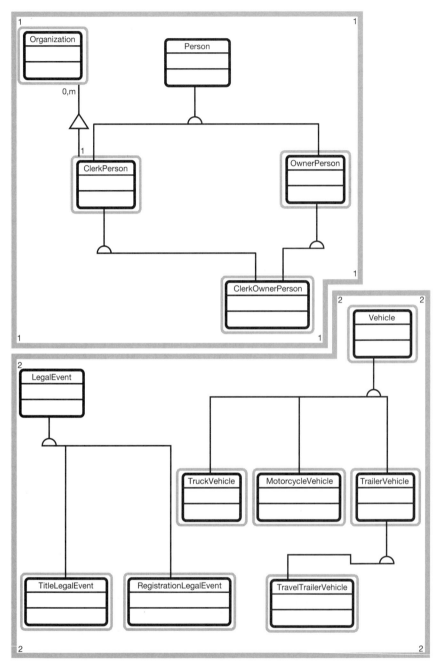

Figure 5.10: Registration and Title System—
Subject, Class-&-Object, and Structure layers

This example uses Mission and Airlift Subjects.

Figure 5.11: Real-Time Airlift System—Subject layer

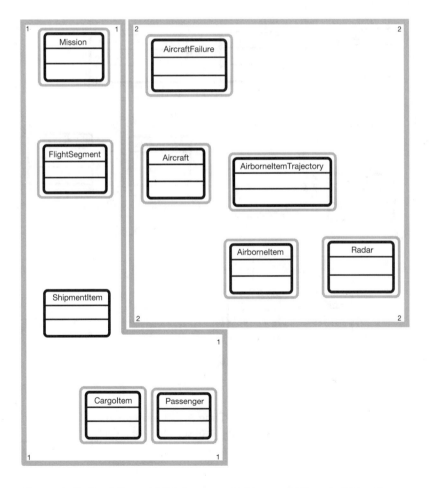

Figure 5.12: Real-Time Airlift System—Subject and Class-&-Object layers

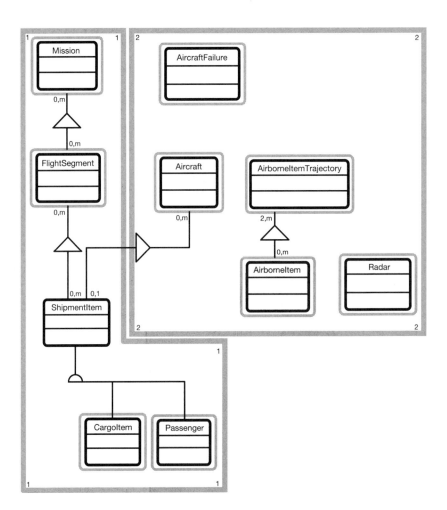

Figure 5.13: Real-Time Airlift System—
Subject, Class-&-Object, and Structure layers

6

Defining Attributes

This chapter examines Attributes—what, why, how, and key points.

6.1 ATTRIBUTES—WHAT

Webster's defines "attribute" with the following:

> Attribute. Any property, quality, or characteristic that can be ascribed to a person or thing.
> [Webster's, 1977]

In OOA, the term "Attribute" is defined reflecting both the problem domain and the system's responsibilities:

> Attribute. An Attribute is some data (state information) for which each Object in a Class has its own value.

Our OOA model is now getting more specific and more detailed. Each Class-&-Object is described in more detail with Attributes; Attributes are described in more detail in a Class-&-Object specification.

6.2 ATTRIBUTES—WHY

Attributes add detail to the "Class-&-Object" and "Structure" abstractions.

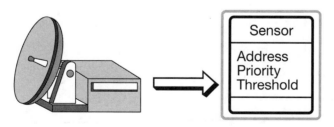

Figure 6.1: Adding details with Attributes

Choosing Attributes involves analysis and choice. For "Sensor," the analyst makes a conscious choice in detailing the abstraction. For example, sensor weight, color, and surface texture, while pertinent in other contexts, are not part of the abstraction chosen in the example. Instead, address, priority, and threshold represent *in this system* in more detail what is meant by the abstraction "Sensor"; Services would use these Attributes (i.e., the state information), perhaps monitoring the actual sensor and producing an alarm notification whenever the threshold is met or exceeded.

Attributes describe values (state) kept within an Object, to be exclusively manipulated by the Services of that Object. We treat Attributes and exclusive Services on those Attributes as an intrinsic whole. If another part of the system needs to access or otherwise manipulate the values in an Object, it must do so by specifying a Message Connection corresponding to a Service defined for that Object. In OOA, this is a specification discipline, with narrow, well-defined interfaces between portions of the overall specification. And so, encapsulation and data abstraction come into play as we move along in the OOA method.

Note that, over time, the problem domain Classes remain quite stable. However, Attributes are more likely to change. For example, consider an "Aircraft" Class within the problem domain of air traffic control. Currently, certain aircraft transmit both identification and altitude. Several years from now, certain aircraft will report a much broader bandwidth of data, including such things as rate of climb/descent, aileron positions, and on-board sub-system status; the system on the ground may know (by aileron positions) when an aircraft is turning, rather than having to guess (extrapolate) with radar returns only, as is done today. The "Aircraft" Class will remain, but the number of Attributes (and the sophistication of the exclusive Services on those Attributes) will change.

6.3 ATTRIBUTES—HOW

Define Attributes by applying the following:

- Identify the Attributes
- Position the Attributes
- Identify Instance Connections
- Check for Special Cases
- Specify the Attributes

Notation

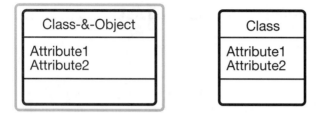

Figure 6.2: Attribute notation

Attributes are placed in the center section of the Class-&-Object and Class symbols.

6.3.1 Identify the Attributes

Questions to ask

What is the Object in a Class responsible for knowing? Responsibilities are the key issue. Ask, from the perspective of a single Object:

- "How am I described in general?"
- "How am I described in this problem domain?"
- "How am I described in the context of this system's responsibilities?"

  Followed by:

- "What do I need to know?"
- "What state information do I need to remember over time?
- "What states can I be in?"

Also, check previous OOA results in the same and similar problem domains. Which Attributes can be directly reused? What lessons can be learned for defining Attributes pertinent to the system under consideration?

For example, consider a human being who plays a role of interest to the system under consideration. What attributes of that human being should the system keep track of?

Name

Address

Title

Figure 6.3: Selecting Attributes pertinent to
the problem domain and the system's responsibilities

For a Class-&-Object called "Supervisor," the problem domain
and the system's responsibilities dictate the appropriate Attributes.
This means that we have a new opportunity to discuss system
context—in other words, what does the system need to know about
a supervisor?

Some Attributes are fairly straightforward—name, address, and
title, perhaps. But, of course, many more Attributes are possible for a
"Supervisor," or for that matter, other human beings.

For example, both authors travel around the country and the
world on consulting assignments at a pace that most people would
consider unusual, if not downright insane. One of the authors recently used his credit card in a part of the world he had not previously
traveled to. In a matter of days, his credit card company sent him a
form letter saying, "By the way, we noticed your card being used in
a place we're not used to seeing it used. Is everything OK? Is your card
stolen?"

This concern indicated that their system was keeping track of
information and providing processing about us that we don't believe
is any of their business. Eventually, they could monitor the fact that
we buy flowers on the opposite side of town from where we live, and
try to make some sort of conclusions. Invasion of privacy? Ethical
considerations? Nonetheless, the analyst who developed that credit
card system had to decide what Attributes were needed for the
system to meet its desired objectives.

Another example is a Class-&-Object called "Aircraft." What
detailed information must be known about that actual aircraft? Perhaps altitude, cruising speed, and maximum rate of ascent?

Atomic concept

Make each Attribute capture an "atomic concept," meaning a single value or a tightly-related grouping of values. This concept may be an individual data element (e.g., driver's license number), or it may be a natural grouping of data elements (e.g., legal name: the composite of first name, middle initial, and last name; or address: the composite of street, city, state, mailing code, and country). The motivation for expressing an "atomic concept" is to produce a simpler model for human review, with fewer Attribute names, and natural data groupings for easier assimilation; the reader focuses on the fact that an Address is captured, rather than scanning the list of Attributes to determine whether each tightly-related piece is somewhere in the list of Attributes. "Name" and "Address" better represent what is being captured.

Deferred to design—normalization

Deferred to design are the compromises between introducing new tables to eliminate data redundancy (normalization) and achieving acceptable performance. For design, normalization requires that each data element have no internal structure (this rule is part of putting data into first normal form). But this normalization is not the analyst's concern as he builds the initial model. Indeed, at this early stage, there is no realistic way of knowing whether the designer will choose to normalize the data—and if so, what level of normalization will be achieved.

Deferred to design—identification mechanisms

Also deferred to design is the selection of actual identification mechanisms, e.g., keys, correlation tables, pointers.

Identification Attributes provide a convenient means of referencing an Object and its connections to other Objects.

Every Object needs such identifiers. So as a convention to keep the diagrams simpler, each Object has an implicit identifier (*id*, for "identifier") and connection identifiers (*cid*, for "connection identifier(s)"). These identifiers are "implicit," which means that they are not explicitly shown on the OOA Attribute layer.

The primary reason for denoting these identifiers is convenience in specifying Services—i.e., to simplify identifying a specific Object or a connection between Objects within a specification.

Another reason for using implicit identification Attributes is to avoid selecting "real-world" identifiers—ones the system is unable to issue directly—as unique identifiers. A unique identifier must be unique and must not change once it is in the system. This isolation means making some design choices, because real-world identifiers cannot be guaranteed unique. For example, in a vehicle registration system, Vehicle Identification Numbers (VINs) might appear to be unique. One could use VIN instead of "id" for identifying an Object; but real-world identifiers have duplicates. A clerk might enter an incorrect VIN; some time later another clerk might try to enter the legitimate but duplicate of that number. Even worse, in some regions, an individual can build his own trailer, put whatever VIN on it he desires, and get it registered. Moreover, that same individual can come in again with another trailer, with the same VIN on it (perhaps it has some special significance to him, like a winning lottery ticket number, or the date he graduated from college), and register that trailer too. So, even if manufacturers don't make mistakes (a bad assumption), the problem domain still presents the potential for duplicate VINs.

Another example: in the United States, Social Security numbers seem unique enough, assuming we could ignore clerical errors (which is a bad assumption, because American Social Security numbers, unlike those in other countries, do not contain embedded check digits). And, because so many real-world systems *do* use Social Security number as an identifier, the typical analyst would assume that it's a safe choice—until he discovers that the numbers get recycled. Depending upon the problem domain (e.g., a banking system) and the longevity of Objects in that domain, this potential duplication could be a serious problem.

Rather than use a real-world identifier (e.g., VIN) and a tie-breaker (e.g., VINTieBreaker) in analysis work (ugh!)—complicating the model and adding detail that is design-specific and possibly design-in-error—use the implicit identifiers ("id" and "cid") as convenient "handles" for referring to an Object. Then at design time, choose between a multi-Attribute key (real-world identifier plus a tie-breaker) and a single Attribute key that can be guaranteed to be unique (one that the system itself generates).

Deferred to design—holding a recalculable Attribute over time

Also deferred to design is the issue of whether an always-recalculable Attribute is held over time. This is typically a tradeoff between CPU time and memory constraints. For OOA, just specify the calculation Service, and not a corresponding always-recalculable Attribute.

For example, consider the calculation of month-to-date fees. The design choices are (1) calculate from scratch each day, or (2) calculate using a "running total" variable held over from the previous day. The "running total" approach represents a "batching" of processing results. For OOA, specify the calculation required (Calculate-MonthToDateFees), but not the recalculable interim result (no Attribute called RunningTotal).

6.3.2 Position the Attributes

Put each Attribute within the Class-&-Object which it best describes; check the problem domain. In most cases, this correspondence is fairly straightforward—e.g., a vehicle has the Attributes Year and BodyStyle. But when it's a close call—i.e., when it's not clear which Class-&-Object should own a particular Attribute—look back at the problem domain itself. What does the Attribute *really* describe? Model the reality. The rationale: maximum stability and modeling consistency.

For example, in a vehicle registration and title system, the vehicle color might be significant (although present laws do not allow such information to be kept). But where does the Attribute "color" belong? Vehicle color is going to be captured at the time the vehicle is registered. Does this addition mean that "color" describes a registration event, or a vehicle? Color really is descriptive of a vehicle (it's painted a particular color)—even though the information is captured at registration or possibly some other time (e.g., shortly after it's been seen at the scene of a crime). So the Attribute "Color" describes a Vehicle.

For Classes within a Gen-Spec Structure, put an Attribute at the uppermost point in the Structure in which it remains applicable to each of its specializations. If an Attribute applies across an entire level of specializations, then move it up to the corresponding generalization instead.

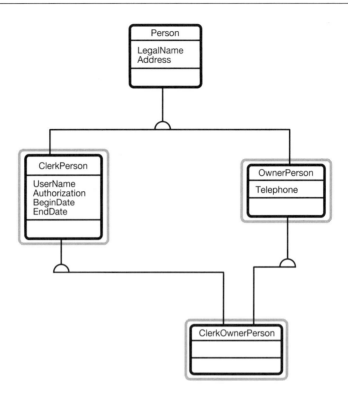

Figure 6.4: Positioning the Attributes

If you find a situation where an Attribute sometimes has a meaningful value, but sometimes its value is "not applicable" or "it just doesn't apply here," review the Gen-Spec Structure strategy, checking to see if you've uncovered another Gen-Spec Structure.

6.3.3 Identify Instance Connections

Attributes depict Object state. Instance Connections add to that information, with required mappings needed by an Object to fulfill its responsibilities.

Instance Connections model association, a principle for managing complexity. Webster's defines "association" with the following:

Association. The union or connection of ideas.

[Webster's, 1977]

People use association to tie together certain things that happen at some point in time or under similar circumstances. For OOA, the term "Instance Connection" is defined reflecting both the problem domain and the system's responsibilities:

Instance Connection. An Instance Connection is a model of problem domain mapping(s) that one Object needs with other Objects, in order to fulfill its responsibilities.

Notation

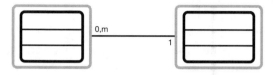

Figure 6.5: Instance Connection notation

An Instance Connection is shown with a line drawn between Objects. The endpoints of an Instance Connection line are positioned to reflect mappings between individual Objects (rather than between Classes).

Each Object has amount (m) or range (m,n) markings on each of its Instance Connections, reflecting its constraints with other Objects. Using an amount or range, rather than ratios, shows the number or range of mappings that may occur. Explicit lower and upper bounds may be directly shown, e.g., "1,5." And if a fixed number of connections must occur, then a single amount can be used (e.g., "1," when one and only one connection is required).

Figure 6.6: Instance Connection example

For example, a particular flight plan must be filed for exactly one aircraft; any particular aircraft may have filed between zero and many flight plans. (Literally: A flight plan has one Instance Connection to a particular aircraft. An aircraft has from zero to many Instance Connections to flight plan(s).)

Since the Class-&-Objects reflect the problem domain and the system's responsibilities within it, we see no need to label an Instance Connection line. Yet optionally, one could do so. It's part of a continual tradeoff—notation complexity vs. model understandability.

Strategy

Check previous OOA results in the same and similar problem domains. Which Instance Connections can be directly reused? What lessons can be learned for defining Instance Connections pertinent to the system under consideration?

For each Object, add connection lines from it to other Objects, reflecting mappings within the problem domain and within the system's responsibilities. Connect to a Gen-Spec Structure at the uppermost applicable level of generalization-specialization.

Add subject-matter mappings between Objects, paying attention to where the connection goes on Gen-Spec Structures.

For each Object, define the amount or range of connections, from the perspective of each Object.

- The lower bound.
    Optional? Lower bound is 0.
    Mandatory? Lower bound is 1 or greater.
- The upper bound.
    Single? Upper bound is 1.
    Multiple? Upper bound is greater than 1.

For an upper bound greater than one, check to see whether certain connected Objects might have special meaning (e.g., the most recent one, the officially approved one); if so, then add an Attribute (e.g., DateTime, ApprovalStatus) to the connected Object's corresponding Class-&-Object symbol.

If constraints apply across more than one Instance Connection attached to a single Object, those constraints may be described in a Class-&-Object specification template section called "additional-Constraints."[1]

Note that we similarly constrain Whole-Part Structures. The difference between Whole-Part Structure and Instance Connection is the underlying semantic strength. Whole-and-part is one of the basic methods of organization that pervade all human thinking. This is much stronger in meaning than a mere mapping between Objects in a Problem Domain.

6.3.4 Check for Special Cases

As you add Attributes and Instance Connections, check for special cases. This section presents a number of checkpoints.

6.3.4.1 Special Cases with Attributes

Check each Attribute for a value of "not applicable."
As mentioned earlier in this chapter, if you find a situation

---

[1] See Chapter 7 for more details.

where an Attribute sometimes has a meaningful value, but sometimes has a value of "not applicable" or "it just doesn't apply here," revisit the Gen-Spec Structure strategy, checking to see whether you've uncovered another Gen-Spec Structure.

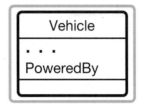

Figure 6.7: Attribute with value "not applicable"

For example, the PoweredBy Attribute may have the values of petrol, diesel, propane, or electric. Yet what if PoweredBy could have the value of "Not Applicable" for certain Objects in a Class (e.g., a standard trailer, which has no engine at all)? When this is the case, revisit the Gen-Spec Structure strategy, checking for an additional generalization-specialization not yet in the model.

Check each Class-&-Object with just one Attribute.

One of the basic methods of organization that pervade huamn thinking is "objects and their attributes." Yet what happens when one finds a Class-&-Object with just one Attribute? It's one of the following:

1. An abstraction of something in the problem domain, in which the system's responsibilities include only a single Attribute—this is just fine.

2. An Attribute of another Class-&-Object, which is out of place in the model.

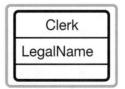

Figure 6.8: Placing a single Attribute within the Class-&-Object it describes

An example of a Class-&-Object with a single Attribute is this Clerk Class-&-Object, whose only Attribute is LegalName. If this captures the system's responsibilities for a clerk, then it's just fine.

Yet when an Attribute is out of place in the model, the model itself can be simplified by placing that Attribute within the Class-&-Object it really describes.

Figure 6.9: Placing a single Attribute within the Class-&-Object it describes

For example, Address is actually an Attribute of the Lien (the loan made for a vehicle). Again, we check the problem domain. The Class-&-Object can be more simply shown with a single symbol, as shown on the right.

Check each Attribute for repeating values.

Look for (potentially) repeating Attribute values. If an Attribute has repeating values, revisit the "Finding Class-&-Objects" strategy—you may uncover an additional Class-&-Object, corresponding to the problem domain reality represented by the Attribute with repeating values.

Figure 6.10: Attributes with repeating values

In the example on the left, an Owner Class-&-Object has been identified. Yet the VIN Attribute has potentially repeating values. Further investigation may uncover another Class-&-Object, perhaps not recognized until this point: a "Vehicle" Class-&-Object, qualifying under the Class-&-Object criteria of "other system" and "thing remembered."

6.3.4.2   Special Cases with Instance Connections

Check each many-to-many Instance Connection.

A many-to-many Instance Connection has upper bound ranges greater than one on each end. For such a connection, ask what Attributes might describe the connection.

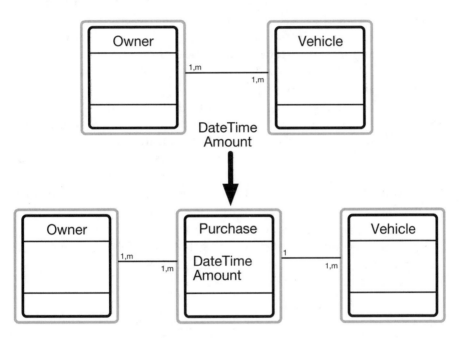

Figure 6.11: Many-to-many Instance Connections

For example, consider the Instance Connection between Owner and Vehicle. What about DateTime and Amount? These Attributes describe the interaction at some point in time between an owner and a vehicle. When this is the case, add an "event remembered" Purchase Class-&-Object to the model.

Note that the end result is not the banishing of all many-to-many connections. Instead, look for this pattern in the model, and check for additional "event remembered" Class-&-Objects.

Check each Instance Connection between Objects of a single Class.

Figure 6.12: Instance Connection between Objects of a Single Class

An Instance Connection may occur between Objects of a Single Class. For such a connection, ask what might describe the mapping.

If a mapping is simple in meaning, e.g., an owner is married to another, then just the Instance Connection, along with a description of it in the "additionalConstraints" section of the Class-&-Object specification, is sufficient.

Yet even if a mapping appears simple in meaning, check to see whether an "event remembered" Class-&-Object is needed, to capture more details about that mapping, e.g., information pertinent to those owners at the time they became spouses (date and time, address, person presiding, legal certificate number, and the like—all interesting Attributes, when pertinent to the system's responsibilities).

Check multiple Instance Connections between Objects.

What if more than one mapping between Objects is needed? Multiple mappings imply some semantic distinction, capturable with another "event remembered" Class-&-Object.

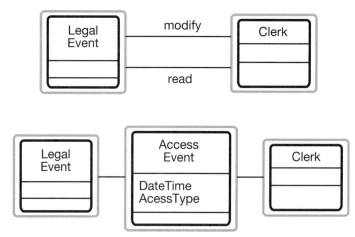

Figure 6.13: Multiple Instance Connections between Objects

In this example, suppose that a Legal Event Object knows about its connections to each Clerk Object corresponding to a "read" or a "modify." For a system responsible for not only the mapping, but also the distinction between a "read" and a "modify," an AccessEvent Class-&-Object is needed, to capture the added semantics of the different mappings between legal events and clerks.

Check for additional needed Instance Connections.

Consider each pair of Objects. Ask the following questions:

- Is a mapping in the problem domain? Within the system's responsibilities?

- Is that mapping always available by traversing other Instance Connections? If so, then do not add another Instance Connection; go with a simpler model. If not, then add the needed connection.

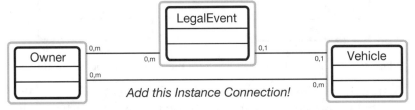

Figure 6.14: Object with more than one optional connection

In this example, a LegalEvent Object may have a connection to both an Owner and a Vehicle. If a Vehicle and Owner can exist without a corresponding LegalEvent, and the system is responsible for that mapping, then add the additional Instance Connection, as shown.

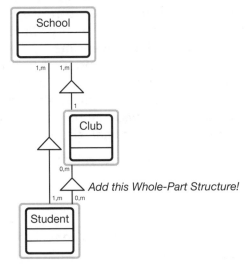

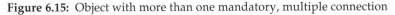

Figure 6.15: Object with more than one mandatory, multiple connection

This example applies a similar concept to Whole-Part Structure (it's also a mapping, but much stronger in underlying semantic content). A school has connections to student(s). A school also has connections to club(s). Yet to capture which student is in which club, an additional mapping (directly between student and club) is needed.

Check for one connecting Object (of many) having special meaning.

When one connecting Object has special meaning (e.g., the most recent one, the officially approved one), add an Attribute to the affected Class-&-Object symbol (e.g., DateTime, ApprovalStatus).

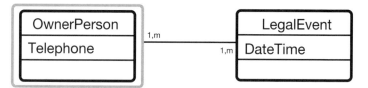

Figure 6.16: One connecting Object (of many) having special meaning

Here, for an OwnerPerson Object, the most recent LegalEvent Object that it maps to is distinguished by the corresponding value of the DateTime Attribute.

6.3.5 Specify the Attributes

Carefully name each Attribute. Use the standard vocabulary for the problem domain and the system's responsibilities in that domain. Use readable names (avoid specially-coded prefixes or suffixes and avoid all-capital terms; both are harder to read). Stay away from embedding values into the name (e.g., choose "PoweredBy" rather than "Diesel")—simply too volatile over time.

Then add a one- or two-line description of each Attribute.

Under the scrutiny of cost-benefit, consider adding constraints to the specification of each Attribute. A constraint may pay for itself, if the effort of it simplifies or reduces the Service specification effort. Additional constraints pertinent to analysis include:

- Unit of measure, range, limit, enumeration
- Precision
- Default value
- Required
  Is a value for this Attribute required to be set?
- Create or access constraints
  Under what conditions are create and access Services allowed?

- Constraints by other Attribute values
  What impact do other Attribute values have on this one?
- Traceability code(s)
  How does this Attribute trace back to the "requesting document" for this project?
- Applicable state code(s)[2]
  What states does this Attribute apply in?

Specify Attributes with names and descriptions. Depending upon what helps to understand the description, what's required by the client, what you can justify in terms of reduced Service specification length, or other factors, you may also add certain Attribute constraints.

Using part of the Class-&-Object specification template described in Chapter 7, here is an example of specifying Attributes:

specification Sensor
attribute Model: the manufacturer and model number
attribute InitSequence: the initialization sequence
attribute Conversion: consists of scale factor, bias, and unit of
    measure
attribute Interval: the sampling interval for this sensor
attribute Address: the address for this sensor
attribute Threshold: the alarm threshold value
attribute State: the state of operation for this sensor (off, standby,
    monitor)
attribute Value: the most recently read and converted value of the
    Sensor, in conversion units of measure

6.4 ATTRIBUTES—KEY POINTS

Summarizing the "Defining Attributes" activity:

NOTATION—Defining Attributes

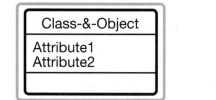 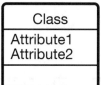

Figure 6.17: Attribute notation

[2] Such information (e.g., traceability codes, applicable state codes) may even be put on the Attribute and Service layers themselves, for heightened visibility.

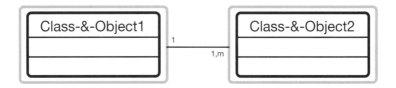

Figure 6.18: Instance Connection notation

STRATEGY—Defining Attributes

Attribute. An Attribute is some data (state information) for which each Object in a Class has its own value.

Identify Attributes

Questions to ask.

"How am I described in general?"

"How am I described in this problem domain?

"How am I described in the context of this system's responsbilities?"

"What do I need to know?"

"What state information do I need to remember over time?"

"What states can I be in?"

Check previous OOA results in the same and similar problem domains.

Make each Attribute capture an "atomic concept."

A single value

A tightly-related grouping of values

Put each Attribute with the Class-&-Object it best describes (check the problem domain).

Whether or not an always-recalculable Attribute is held over time is a design decision—time vs. memory. Specify the calculation Service, without a corresponding always-recalculable Attribute.

Implicit identifiers, "id" (identifier) and "cid" (connection identifier), may be used in specification text when needed.

Apply inheritance in Gen-Spec Structures

Position the more general Attributes higher.

Position specialized Attributes lower.

Instance Connection. An Instance Connection is a model of problem domain mapping(s) that one Object needs with other Objects, in order to fulfill its responsibilities.

Check previous OOA results in the same and similar problem domains.

For each Object, add connection lines.

Add subject-matter mappings between Objects, paying attention to where the connection goes on Gen-Spec Structures.

For each Object, define the amount or range.

The lower bound

Optional connection? Lower bound is 0.

Mandatory connection? Lower bound is 1 or greater.

The upper bound

Single connection? Upper bound is 1.

Multiple connections? Upper bound is greater than 1.

(Note: a multiple connection may imply an Attribute to keep track of the current or most recent mapping, e.g., DateTime or Status.)

Use the specification template keyword "additional Constraints" to capture additional constraints, as needed.

Constrain Whole-Part Structures, too. (The difference is the underlying semantic strength.)

Check special cases

Special Cases with Attributes

Check each Attribute for a value of "not applicable."

Check each Class-&-Object with just one Attribute.

Check each Attribute for repeating values.

Special Cases with Instance Connections

Check each many-to-many Instance Connection.

Check each Instance Connection between Objects of a single Class.

Check multiple Instance Connections between Objects.

Check for additional needed Instance Connections.

Check for one connecting Object (of many) having special meaning.

Specify the Attributes

> Name. (Standard vocabulary. Reflects problem domain, system's responsibilities. Readable. No embedded values.)
> Description.
> Constraints.
>> On constraints
>>> May reduce the amount of Service specification needed.
>>> Scrutinize cost vs. benefit.
>> Unit of measure, range, limit, enumeration; default; precision
>> Create/access constraint?
>> Constrained by other Attributes?
>> Traceability code(s), applicable state code(s)
>> (Option: show such code(s) on the Attribute Layer, for heightened visibility.)

EXAMPLE—Sensor System

Each Sensor has a state associated with it, that is, information which is required to be held over time. Some of the Attributes seldom change in value (Model, InitSequence, Conversion), others change more often (Interval, Address, Threshold, State), and others are quite dynamic (Value). The system is responsible for holding this state information—the actual values for each Object—over time.

Note the Attribute called Value. It is the result of reading a value in raw physical units (e.g., volts) and converting it to a standard unit of measure. It could be treated as a recalculable value (at any point, I can just go out and read it); in this case, the Attribute is not needed. Yet the system may be responsible for knowing the value regardless of the state of the sensor (e.g., the last known value read from the sensor, even though it may be in Standby state at the moment, and cannot be read). The Attribute is not always recalculable; in this case, the Attribute is needed.

Also note than a CriticalSensor Object inherits all the Attributes defined for Sensor, and extends the system's responsibilities with the Tolerance Attribute.

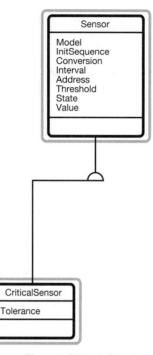

Figure 6.19: Sensor System—Class-&-Object, Structure, and Attribute layers

EXAMPLE—Registration and Title System

Note the Attributes, and the impact of inheritance within the Gen-Spec Structures. For example, a ClerkOwnerPerson Object is described by values for LegalName, Address, UserName, Authorization, BeginDate, EndDate, and Telephone.

Observe that no Fee Attribute is included in LegalEvent. It's an always-recalculable result. Instead, a CalculateFee Service is placed on the Service layer, as shown in Chapter 7.

Also, observe the Instance Connections. From LegalEvent, Instance Connections map out to OwnerPerson, Vehicle, and ClerkPerson. Remember, for each LegalEvent, a ClerkPerson is held account-able for that conducting that legal transaction (and for collecting the corresponding fee).

Even though Whole-Part Structure does not express generalization-specialization (nor inheritance), it is true that certain Attributes which apply to the whole (e.g., Address, in Organization) may apply to the parts (e.g., ClerkPerson). Why? Because the whole and the parts are in close proximity to each other. But that's all—no generalization-specialization (and no inheritance) applies.

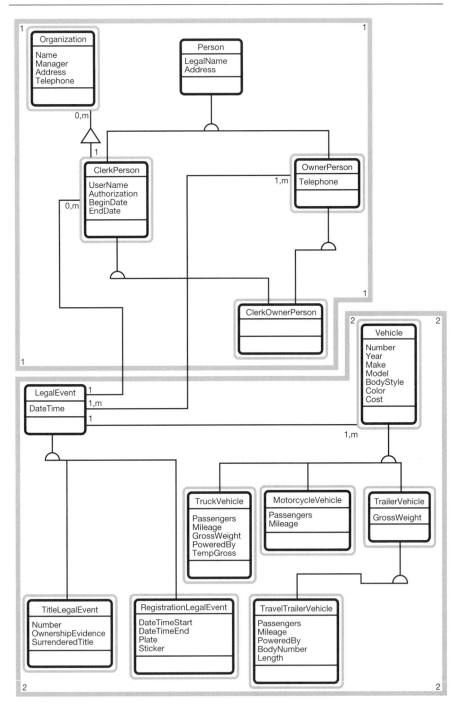

Figure 6.20: Registration and Title System—
Subject, Class-&-Object, Structure, and Attribute layers

EXAMPLE—Real-Time Airlift System

Note the Attributes, and the impact of inheritance within the ShipmentItem Gen-Spec Structure. For example, a Passenger Object is described by values for Number, Origin, NowAt, Destination, Name, and Rank.

Observe AirborneItemTrajectory. It has just one Attribute, because the system's responsibilities only include a single Attribute. And this is just fine.

Also, observe the Instance Connections. From Aircraft, Instance Connections map out to FlightSegment, AircraftFailure, and AirborneItemTrajectory.

Note that no Instance Connection is shown between Radar and AirborneItem. This indicates that the mapping between a particular Radar and a specific AirborneItem is not of interest, given the system's responsibilities. However, if the algorithm to calculate an airborne item trajectory needed such a mapping, or if someone wanted to access the values of an AirborneItem Object and determine its corresponding Radar Object, then an Instance Connection between AirborneItem and Radar would be necessary.

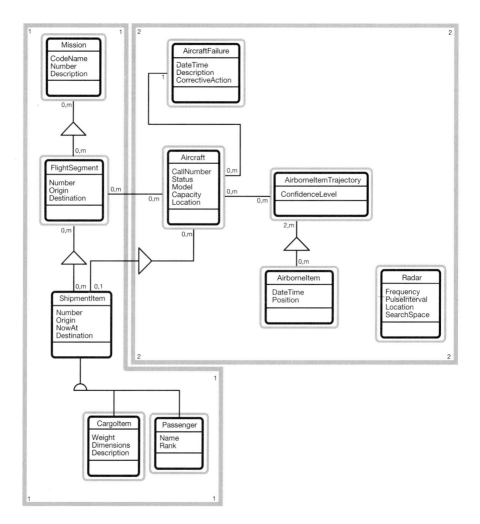

Figure 6.21: Real-Time Airlift System—
Subject, Class-&-Object, Structure, and Attribute layers

7

Defining Services

This chapter examines Services—what, why, how, and key points.

One theme underlying Object-Oriented Analysis is that eventually the analyst must provide a detailed description of a system's processing and sequencing requirements. These highly volatile subjects are recognized for their importance, yet deferred. Rather than jumping right into a study of functions and sequencing, the OOA analyst focuses on Class-&-Objects, Structures, and Attributes—and then proceeds to a fuller consideration of Services.

7.1 SERVICES—WHAT

Webster's defines "service" with the following:

> Service. An activity carried on to provide people with the use of something.
> [Webster's, 1977]

In OOA, the term "Service" is defined to reflect both the problem domain and the system's responsibilities:

> Service. A Service is a specific behavior that an Object is responsible for exhibiting.

The central issue in defining Services is to define required behavior. *Encyclopaedia Britannica* presents three ways of classifying behavior:

> Three types of behavior classification are used most commonly:
> (1) on the basis of immediate causation,
> (2) on similarity of evolutionary history [change over time], and
> (3) on the similarity of function.
> [Britannica, "Animal Behaviour," 1986]

These principles are incorporated in the strategies presented in this chapter. Specifically:

- "Object States" builds upon the principle of "change over time."
- "Required Services" builds upon the principles of "similarity of function" and "immediate causation."

A second issue in defining Services is to define the necessary communication between Objects. Such commands and requests are the very nature of human interaction with a system. And the very same interaction paradigm is used between parts of the OOA model.

Services and Message Connections are specified in the Class-&-Object specifications, establishing the observable, measurable processing requirements.

Strategies for identifying Services and Message Connections, and developing the corresponding specifications, are presented in this chapter.

7.2 SERVICES—WHY

Services further detail the abstraction of the reality being modeled, indicating what behavior will be provided by an Object within a Class.

Ultimately, every data processing system must have "data" and "processing." Our discussion in the previous chapter focused on the data in a system. Now we describe the functional processing that is to take place upon that data.

7.3 SERVICES—HOW

The strategy for defining Services has these activities:

- Identify Object States
- Identify the required Services
- Identify Message Connections
- Specify the Services
- Put the OOA documentation set together

Some analysts prefer to work from Attributes to Services. Others prefer to work from Services to Attributes. We think both perspectives are valuable; we tend to work back and forth between the activities during this more detailed part of OOA. For the sake of presentation, this chapter is organized in an Attributes-to-Services manner.

Notation

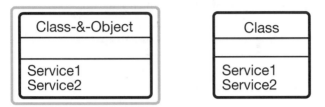

Figure 7.1: Service notation

Services are placed in the bottom section of the Class-&-Object and Class symbols.

7.3.1 Identify the Object States

Each Object goes through different states, from the time it is created until the time it is released (deleted, zapped). The state of an Object is represented by the values of its Attributes. Every change in Attribute value(s) reflects a change in state.

An Object State is the identification of Attribute value(s) which reflects a change in Object behavior. To identify Object States, (1) examine the potential values for the Attributes and (2) determine whether the system's responsibilities include different behavior for those potential values.

Also, check previous OOA results in the same and similar problem domains. Which Object States can be directly reused? What lessons can be learned for identifying Object States pertinent to the system under consideration?

For example, consider the Attributes in the Sensor System. Which Attribute values reflect a needed change in Object behavior?

The Attributes are Model, InitSequence, Conversion, Interval, Address, Threshold, State, and Value. Which values imply a change in behavior? This depends upon the system's responsibilities. In this system, the values of Model, InitSequence, Conversion, Interval, Address, and Threshold do not imply a change of behavior. It is important to realize that they could, e.g., special behavior defined for various model values. In this system, the Attribute called "State" is the one which reflects a needed change in behavior; its values are "off," "standby," and "on."

Object State Diagrams present the different states or modes of an Object over time. The chart identifies the states and transitions from one state to another; the detailed behavior and changes in behavior are defined within the specification of the Services.

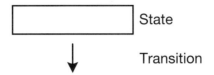

State

Transition

Figure 7.2: Object State Diagram notation

So, continuing with the Sensor System:

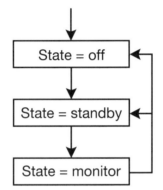

Figure 7.3: An example Object State Diagram

In this example, the top arrow indicates the initial state. Note that only states and legal transitions are shown. The actual state transitions and state behaviors are specified within the specification of the Services, discussed later in this chapter.

7.3.2 Identify the Required Services

This section presents how to identify the required Services—both algorithmically-simple ones and algorithmically-complex ones.

Algorithmically-Simple Services

Algorithmically-simple Services apply to each Class-&-Object in the model. And they follow the same basic pattern, over and over and over again. For example:

Create (a sensor)
- Let me check the value of Model...
- Let me check the value of InitSequence...

- Let me check the value of Conversion...
- Let me check the value of Interval...
- Let me check the value of Address...
- Let me check the value of Threshold...
- If all is well, I'll create and initialize a new Object.
- I'll return the result.

If the Attributes are defined, with whatever constraints are necessary to reflect the problem domain and the system's responsibilities, then such Services can be specified once, describing how to create/initialize an Object. For example:

Create (an Object)
- Let me check the values against the constraints.
- If all is well, I'll create and initialize a new Object.
- I'll return the result.

A more formal version of this Service, using a Service Chart, is presented later in this chapter.

Such a Service may be specified once, and treated as an implicit Service. These Services are "implicit," which means that they are not explicitly shown on the OOA Service layer. Moreover, Message Connections solely depicting interaction between implicit Services are also treated implicitly on the Service layer. And when referred to in other Class-&-Object specifications, these implicit Services are referred to in all-lowercase letters (i.e., create, connect, access, and release).

The four algorithmically-simple Services are Create, Connect, Access, and Release.

Create. This Services creates and initializes a new Object in a Class (this Service is documented in a Class[1]).

Connect. This Service connects (disconnects) an Object with another. In effect, this Service establishes or breaks a mapping between one Object and another.

---

[1] The convention of using a Class as a convenient point of documenting how to create and initialize a new object is useful (but not sacred!). It's useful because (a) the Attribute constraints for such a Service are defined with that Class-&-Object symbol in an OOA model, and (b) it establishes a consistent way of modeling object creation in an OOA model.

Access. This Service gets or sets the Attribute values of an Object.

Release. This Service releases (disconnects and deletes) an Object.

The majority of required behavior in systems is captured in create/connect/access/release. Examples:

- Registration and title systems:
    the algorithmically-simple Services cover at least 95% of the system behavior.
- Mobile telephone communications systems:
    the algorithmically-simple Services cover at least 90% of the system behavior.
- Air traffic control systems:
    the algorithmically-simple Services cover at least 80% of the system behavior.

The other Services are those which are algorithmically complex (and for that matter, algorithmically interesting!).

Algorithmically-Complex Services

Certain Services go beyond the algorithmically-simple Services (create, connect, access, release).

The algorithmically-complex Services fall into two categories— Calculate and Monitor.

Calculate. This Service calculates a result from the Attribute values of an Object.

Monitor. This Service monitors an external system or device. It deals with external system inputs and outputs, or with device data acquisition and control. It may need some companion Services, such as Initialize or Terminate.

Use these categories in determining what Services are needed for an Object, beyond the implicit create/connect/access/release Services.

Then examine an Object in its states, and ask:

- What calculations is the Object responsible for performing on its values?
- What monitoring is the Object responsible for doing, in order

to detect and respond to a change in an external system or device, i.e., the required event-response behavior?

In addition, check previous OOA results in the same and similar problem domains. Which algorithmically-complex Services can be directly reused? What lessons can be learned for defining algorithmically-complex Services pertinent to the system under consideration?

Use domain-specific Service names. For the calculation of a legal event fee, use CalculateFee, rather than just Calculate. For the monitoring of a sensor, use MonitorForAlarmCondition, rather than just Monitor.

7.3.3 Identify Message Connections

This section presents Message Connections—what, why, notation, and strategy.

What

Webster's defines "message" with the following:

Message. Any communication, written or oral, sent between persons.

[Webster's, 1977]

In OOA, the term "Message Connection" is defined to reflect both the problem domain and the system's responsibilities:

Message Connection. A Message Connection models the processing dependency of an Object, indicating a need for Services in order to fulfill its responsibilities.

A Message Connection is a mapping of one Object to another Object (or occasionally to a Class, to create a new Object), in which a "sender" sends a message to a "receiver," to get some processing done. The needed processing is named in the sender's Services specification, and is defined in the receiver's Services specification.

This convention is a specification discipline; literal messages of the "Hi, how are you doing?" variety are *not* sent from Object to Object. The benefit of such a discipline is that it creates a very narrow interface between the strong encapsulations of Attributes and exclusive Services on those Attributes.

Message Connections exist solely for the benefit of the Services.

Yet examining Message Connections prior to specifying the Services guides the analyst to considering processing dependencies with other parts of the system, before focusing on his own specification efforts. A first pass at Message Connections grabs many of the key processing dependencies. One would expect to find some additional Message Connections during the course of actually specifying the Services.

Why

Message interaction corresponds to the imperative mood in languages. "The imperative mood conveys commands or requests..." [Britannica, "Imperative Mood," 1986].

A principle for managing complexity—notably for interfaces— is communication with messages.

In effect, a Message Connection combines event-response and data flow perspectives; that is, each Message Connection represents values sent within the context of a particular service need, and a response received as a result.

Notation

The notation for a Message Connection is a light or dashed arrow.

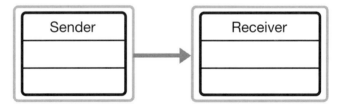

Figure 7.4: Message Connection notation

The arrow points from sender to receiver. The arrow indicates that the sender "sends" a message; the receiver "receives" the message; and the receiver takes some action and returns a result to the sender.[2,3]

---

[2] Note that this diagramming technique carries more meaning than what is represented by a one-directional arrow in a data flow approach.

[3] Generally, the receiver completes the action, *then* returns a result. Yet it's possible in OOA for the receiver to return a result, and then continue to take ongoing action. Also in OOA, a Service can have trigger and terminate constraints, so that it can activate itself without the need for a message to be sent to it.

Each end of the arrow usually connects to an Object (or occasionally to a Class, to create a new Object), to indicate the actual participants.

Threads of execution may be named, defined, and presented using different line patterns for each thread. With CASE tool support, (1) threads of execution may be named, defined, and displayed—one at a time or all together, using different line patterns for each thread—or (2) a Service may be selectable, to see what messages invoke it and what messages it sends.

Document the message sent in the sender's Class-&-Object specification. Document the corresponding Service performed in the receiver's Class-&-Object specification.

In addition, Message Connection lines could be labeled with Service names. It's a tradeoff of notation complexity vs. model understandability. We prefer not to add Service names on the lines, and just let the reader pick up the Message Connection details in the specifications of the participating Class-&-Objects.

For Message Connections emanating from one Object to *many* other Objects, an alternate notation may be used. This notation should be used only when the graphical inclusion of all of the corresponding Message Connections would make the model unreadable.

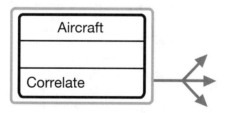

Figure 7.5: Message Connection notation for connections to many Objects

Taking this alternate notation further, what about human interaction with the system? Commands are the very nature of human interaction with a system. And the very same interaction paradigm is used between the parts of an OOA model. Human interaction could be shown on the model too.

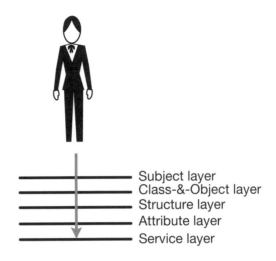

Figure 7.6: Depicting human interaction: a preferred approach

Such interaction runs across nearly all of an OOA model. In fact, the human(s) can be thought of as interacting with the entire model, invoking Services as desired (e.g., create, connect, access, release—provided that access constraints are satisfied!). We prefer this approach.

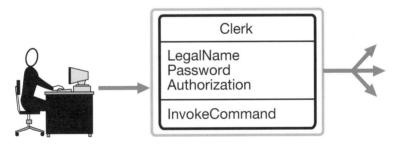

Figure 7.7: Depicting human interaction: an alternative

An alternative approach is to bring the human interaction Message Connections into the model itself, as shown. The multi-headed Message Connection symbol helps here.

Strategy

To identify needed Message Connections, ask, for each Object:

- What other Objects does it need Services from? Draw an arrow to each of those Objects.
- What other Objects need one of its Services? Draw an arrow from each of those Objects to the one under consideration.
- Follow each Message Connection to the next Object, and repeat the questions.

Also, check previous OOA results in the same and similar problem domains. Which Message Connections can be directly reused? What lessons can be learned for defining Message Connections pertinent to the system under consideration?

In applying this strategy, one gets interested in the threads of execution, from one message to the next to the next. Such threads help analysts check for model completeness (via role-playing simulation, by humans or by computer) and determine real-time processing requirements (when pertinent).

These threads of execution can be further analyzed and constrained, especially for real-time systems. "Real-time" analysis means that performance constraints apply, constraining both the timing and sizing of the system under consideration. "Hard real-time" systems have timing constraints which must be met, or otherwise the computational results are of little or no value. ("Real-time" design addresses such issues as task selection, communication, and coordination.)

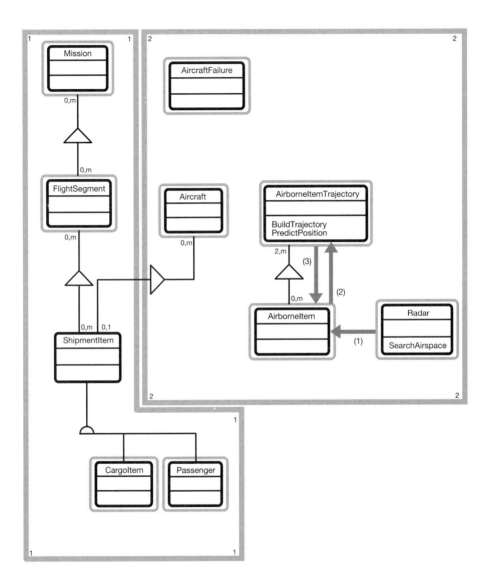

Figure 7.8: Depicting a critical thread of execution

This example depicts a critical thread of execution within the Real-Time Airlift System. The thread itself is shown with the Message Connections and the supporting specification text. In this figure, some added annotations help point out the actual sequence—(1), (2), then (3).

Here's a description of the thread of execution highlighted in this example:

- A user requests that Radar searches an airspace. Radar commands the actual radar. Upon a radar return indicating that something has been found, Radar sends a message to create a new AirborneItem.
- The new AirborneItem sends a message to create a new AirborneItem Trajectory.
- The new AirborneItemTrajectory sends messages to existing AirborneItem(s) to access values. It builds a trajectory, with a corresponding confidence level.

The thread appears in the Class-&-Object specifications, presented in a bullet list format (as shown here) or in Service Chart format (presented in the next section of this chapter):

specification Radar

...

externalInput RadarResponse: the input data from the actual radar.
externalOutput RadarCommand: the command sent out to an actual radar.

service SearchAirspace (in: values; out: result) ...
- shall output a search command to the actual radar (via RadarCommand).
- repeat
  - inputs a response from the actual radar (via RadarResponse).
  - sends the message AirborneItem.create (in: values; out: result).
- until commanded again.

timeRequirements 550 milliseconds from the time it inputs a radar response until the time a corresponding AirborneItem is created and initialized.

specification AirborneItem

...

service create (in: id; out: result)
- creates and initializes, as specified for the implicit "create" Service.
- sends the message Trajectory.create (in: values; out: result).

specification AirborneItemTrajectory

...

service BuildTrajectory ...

• repeat for each AirborneItem, until released

   - sends the message AirborneItem.access (in: id; out: result).

   - computes, and if it fits (algorithm to be determined), adds the AirborneItem to this AirborneItemTrajectory.

timeRequirements 1100 milliseconds from the time a new AirborneItem is added until the time the AirborneItemTrajectory updates itself.

Figure 7.9: A thread of execution

Certain threads of execution may be vital to the system fulfilling its mission. In such a thread, an overall thread budget for the thread can be allocated across the participating Services and Message Connections. This effort requires some assumptions about the implementation technology to be used, as well as some assumptions about how the design parts will interact with the available resources at run time. Simulation (by humans or by computer) can make it possible to consider a wider variety of time budget estimates and implementation assumptions. But the challenge and "guesstimation" of budgeting remain the same.

7.3.4 Specify the Services

Specify the Services within a Class-&-Object template, using a Service Chart for each Service.

specification
   attribute
   attribute
   attribute
   externalInput
   externalOutput
   objectStateDiagram
   additionalConstraints
   notes
   service <name & Service Chart>
   service <name & Service Chart>

service <name & Service Chart>
and, as needed[4],
   traceabilityCodes
   applicableStateCodes
   timeRequirements
   memoryRequirements

Figure 7.10: A Class-&-Object template

Within the template, Service Charts[5] graphically portray the Service requirements.

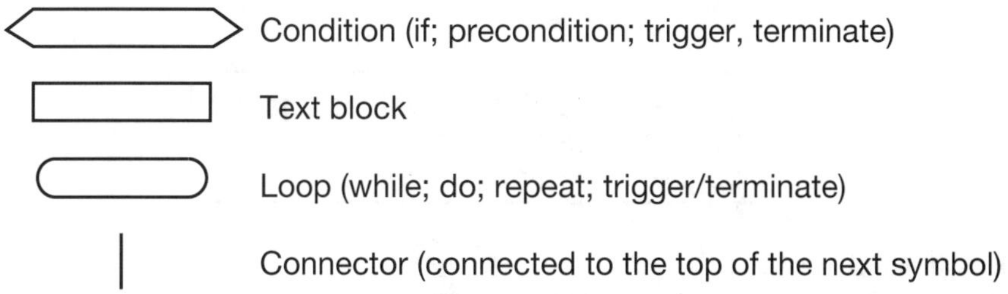

Condition (if; precondition; trigger, terminate)

Text block

Loop (while; do; repeat; trigger/terminate)

Connector (connected to the top of the next symbol)

Figure 7.11: Service Chart notation

Note that Service Charts express state-dependent behavior using precondition, trigger, and terminate.

We use this notation to specify Services. And we've found that, in practice, the Service Chart approach has significantly improved the specification content.

Yet in many ways the Service Chart notation is much like a flow chart. A number of years ago, a client gave one of the authors a complex algorithm from a previous project. A foot-long, finely detailed flow chart, along with pages of equations, defined the algorithm. The flow chart summarized with "do this, then this, then this; based on the result, if it's this value do this, otherwise..." The author thought, "Wow. This is too complex. And the detail is overwhelming.

---

[4] Such information may even be put on the Attribute and Service layers themselves, for heightened visibility.

[5] This is an extension and simplification of a part of George Cherry's notation in Cherry, 1990.

I should build a data flow diagram for this." After days of drawing and re-drawing, the author realized how futile all the effort had been. A data flow diagram is a poor choice for stepping through an algorithm; a flow chart is ideal. Service Chart notation provides a tool for applying the principle of procedural abstraction systematically, within the limited context (scope) of a single Service.

Even in the specifying of Services, check previous OOA results in the same and similar problem domains. Which specifications can be directly reused? What lessons can be learned for specifying Services pertinent to the system under consideration?

An example—create

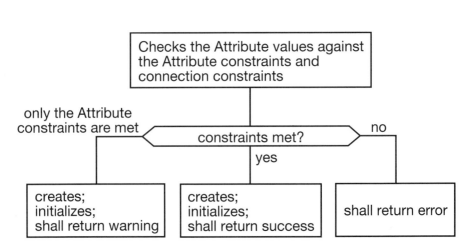

Figure 7.12: A Service Chart for the implicit Service "create"

This first example shows a Service Chart for the implicit Service "create." Remember that an implicit Service is one that is not normally shown on the Service layer. And it is a Service that can be specified one time; it also can be extended as needed, by explicitly naming the Service on the Service layer and then extending the Service in the corresponding specification.

Another example: Sensor and CriticalSensor

Consider the following example, for Sensor and CriticalSensor. Observe how Service Charts express state-dependent behavior using precondition, trigger, and terminate. And note the use of Attribute and Service inheritance in specifying a CriticalSensor.

specification Sensor

    attribute Model: the manufacturer and model number

    attribute InitSequence: the initialization sequence

    attribute Conversion: consists of scale factor, bias, and unit of measure

    attribute Interval: the sampling interval for this sensor

    attribute Address: the address for this sensor

    attribute Threshold: the alarm threshold value

    attribute State: the state of operation for this sensor (off, standby, monitor)

    attribute Value: the most recently read and converted value of the Sensor, in conversion units of measure

    externalInput
       SensorReading: the raw data read from the sensor

    externalOutput
       SensorControl: the control command sent to the sensor

    objectStateDiagram

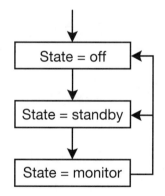

Figure 7.13: Sensor Class-&-Object specification

service Initialize (out: result)

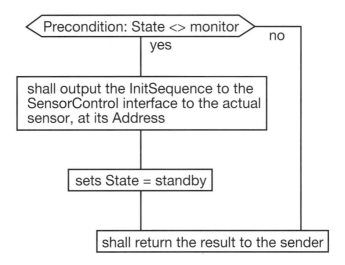

sevice Sample (out: result)

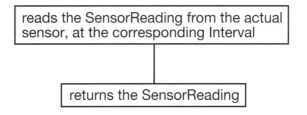

Figure 7.14: Sensor Class-&-Object specification (continued)

service MonitorForAlarmCondition

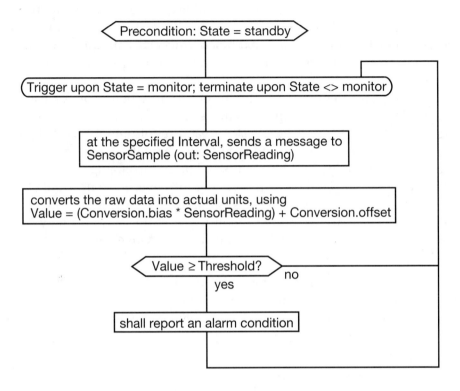

specification CriticalSensor

attribute Tolerance: the sampling interval tolerance for this sensor

service Sample (out: result)

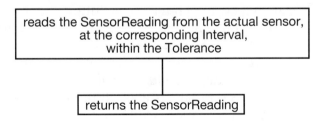

Figure 7.15: Sensor Class-&-Object specification (continued)

Text block style

Use a consistent style in each text block, using either a sentence fragment or a full sentence. Keep just one requirement sentence fragment or full sentence per text block (optionally uniquely identified and cross-referenced to other documents, for requirements traceability purposes).

Specify the required externally observable behavior for each Object. Each time, ask, "Can this requirement be externally observed (tested)?" Consider writing a test for each requirement levied; this discipline helps streamline and focus requirements statements even further, emphasizing testable results and de-emphasizing processing steps, keeping the analyst from straying into over-specification.

Consider using a verb tense systematically, to give special emphasis to externally observable requirements. In fact, you may be required to apply such a discipline for U.S. Government system development.

Absolute tense, third person: it *shall*, they *shall*[6]

This expresses a binding, measurable requirement.

Future tense, third person: he/she *will*, it *will*, they *will*

This expresses a reference to the future.

Present tense

Use this for all other times.

A "shall" requirement is observable when a system is delivered: observing the fulfillment of a requirement in terms of an end result (output) being produced by the system (e.g., "shall report an alarm condition"). Asking the question "Can this requirement be externally observed or tested?" is the key to accurately specifying such a requirement.

A "will" statement simply refers to the future, describing something that will happen, but is not under the control of the system being specified; typically these are human actions beyond system interaction (e.g., "the controller will study the potential aircraft-to-aircraft conflict"), or actions of independently developed systems (e.g., "the independently developed radar system will report error conditions directly to the radar maintenance facility").

---

[6] The distinction between "absolute" and "future" tense is not formally part of modern English. It comes from older forms of English, e.g., "thou shalt be saved."

Use present tense in all other cases.

Services specified with Service Charts keep the textual specification concise and well-focused. Yet certain readers (management, clients, and the like) may want and require extensive volumes of narrative text (referred to as "Victorian novels" or "river rafts"). Fight for Service Charts; they are succinct and drive home observable, measurable requirements.

If narrative text is required and/or desired, get technical writers—professionals with the requisite writing skills—to translate the bullets into narrative. Both the analysts and the writers will be happier with their work assignments and the overall result.

If analysts are required to write narrative specifications, give them time to study *The Elements of Style* [Strunk and White, 1979], *The Elements of Grammar* [Shertzer, 1986], and *Revising Business Prose* [Lanham, 1981]. But listen to your staff; don't let them spend so much time in text refinement that they describe themselves as highly paid clerks (this is definitely a warning sign!). And encourage them to reduce what Lanham calls the "lard factor"; they needn't write in bureaucratese. Even if a client demands bureaucratese—e.g., to fulfill the documentation standards set by a government agency—at least keep the technical work and thoughts clear. (We have met analysts who not only wrote in bureaucratese, but also talked and thought in it. Ugh!)

Expressing Additional Constraints

For real-time systems, performance (timing and sizing) constraints must be specified. For all systems, overall response time, availability, reliability, and other quantified requirements may be specified. Some of these constraints apply to individual Services, and belong in the Service specification; other performance constraints apply system-wide, and may be specified and included in the OOA documentation set.

Summarizing State-Dependent Services

The state dependencies of each Service are specified using "precondition," "trigger," and "terminate." To summarize these state dependencies across the model, you may choose to construct a Services/States Table. This table summarizes the state-dependent behavior detailed in the specification of Services.

	Full Service State	Reduced Capability State	Emergency State
Aircraft.Access Service	•	•	•
Aircraft.Track Service	•		
Radar.Access Service	•	•	
Radar.Search Service	•	•	

Figure 7.16: Services/States table

In this example, the bullets indicate that a service is defined for certain states. Aircraft.Access includes behavior applicable to all states. In contrast, Aircraft.Track includes behavior applicable only to the full service state.

For heightened visibility, consider putting state codes next to the Services on the Service layer itself.

7.3.5 Put the OOA Documentation Set Together

Finally, put the entire documentation set together. The full package contains:

- The Five Layer OOA Model
  Subject, Class-&-Object, Structure, Attribute, Service
- The Class-&-Object specifications
- Supplemental documentation, as needed
  Table of critical threads of execution
  Additional system constraints
  Services/States table

Deciding when the analysis and specification are complete is domain-driven, system-responsibility-driven, and checklist-driven[7]—within the context of schedule and budget constraints.

---

[7] Such a quality checklist may consist of strategy checks (summarized in Appendix A) and model consistency checks (included in Chapter 8).

7.4 SERVICES—KEY POINTS

Summarizing the "Defining Services" activity:

NOTATION—Defining Services

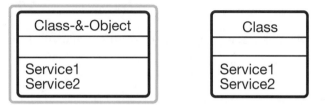

Figure 7.17: Service notation

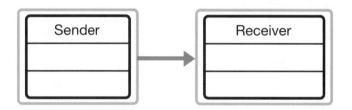

Figure 7.18: Message Connection notation

specification
    attribute
    attribute
    attribute

    externalInput
    externalOutput

    objectStateDiagram

    additionalConstraints

    notes

    service <name & Service Chart>
    service <name & Service Chart>
    service <name & Service Chart>

and, as needed,
    traceabilityCodes
    applicableStateCodes
    timeRequirements
    memoryRequirements

Figure 7.19: Class-&-Object specification template

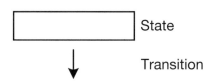

Figure 7.20: Object State Diagram notation (used within the template)

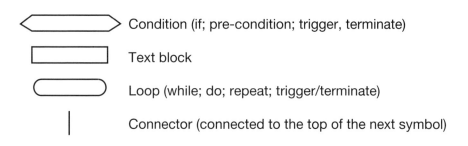

Figure 7.21: Service Chart notation (used within the template, for each Service)

STRATEGY—Defining Services

Service. A Service is a specific behavior that an Object is responsible for exhibiting.

Identify Object States

Examine the potential values for the Attributes.

Determine whether the system's responsibilities include different behavior for those potential values.

Check previous OOA results in the same and similar problem domains.

Describe the states and transitions in an Object State Diagram.

Identify the required Services

Algorithmically-simple Services

Create—creates and initializes a new Object in a Class.

Connect—connects (disconnects) an Object with another.

Access—gets or sets the Attribute values of an Object.

Release—releases (disconnects and deletes) an Object.

Algorithmically-complex Services

Check previous OOA results in the same and similar problem domains.

Two categories

Calculate—calculates a result from the Attribute values of an Object.

Monitor—monitors an external system or device. It deals with external system inputs and outputs, or with device data acquisition and control. It may need some companion Services, such as Initialize or Terminate.

Ask

What calculations is the Object responsible for performing on its values?

What monitoring is the Object responsible for doing, in order to detect and respond to a change in an external system or device, i.e., the required event-response behavior?

Use domain-specific names.

Identify Message Connections

Message Connection. A Message Connection models the processing dependency of an Object, indicating a need for Services in order to fulfill its responsibilities.

For each Object—

What other Objects does it need Services from?

Draw an arrow to each of those Objects.

What other Objects need one of its Services?

Draw an arrow from each of those Objects to the one under consideration.

Follow each Message Connection to the next Object, and repeat the questions.

Check previous OOA results in the same and similar problem domains.

Examine Message Connection threads.

Use to check for model completeness (via role-playing simulation, by humans or by computer).

Use to determine real-time processing requirements (when pertinent)

"Real time" analysis ⇨ performance requirements

Allocate an overall thread budget across the participating Services and Message Connections.

Specify the Services

Check previous OOA results in the same and similar problem domains.

Use a template, with an Object State Diagram and Service Charts.

Use a consistent text block style.

Express additional constraints.

Summarize state-dependent Services using a Services/States table.

For heightened visibility, consider putting state codes next to the Services on the Service layer itself.

Put the OOA documentation set together

The five layer OOA model

The Class-&-Object specifications

Supplemental documentation, as needed

Table of critical threads of execution

Additional system constraints

Services/States table

EXAMPLE—Sensor System

Note the Services and the inheritance of Services in the Sensor Gen-Spec Structure. The Sensor Services are Initialize, Sample, and Monitor. The CriticalSensor Services are Initialize (inherited from Sensor), Sample (inherited from Sensor, and extended in CriticalSensor itself), and MonitorForAlarmCondition (inherited from Sensor).

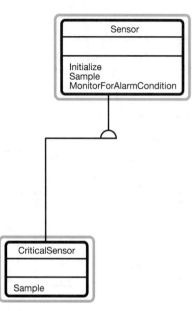

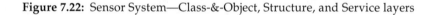

Figure 7.22: Sensor System—Class-&-Object, Structure, and Service layers

EXAMPLE—Registration and Title System

Note that the majority of the symbols in this Service layer have no explicit Services; they all have the implicit Services (create, connect, access, release), not normally shown on the Service layer.

Note the Services and the inheritance of Services in the LegalEvent Gen-Spec Structure. The TitleLegalEvent Services are AcceptFee (inherited) and CalculateFee (inherited and extended). The Registration LegalEvent Services are AcceptFee (inherited), CalculateFee (inherited and extended), and CheckRenewal (an addition; it checks for renewal notification).

Also note the Message Connections. The CalculateFee Service needs to send Access messages to both OwnerPerson and Vehicle in order to fulfill its calculation responsibilities.

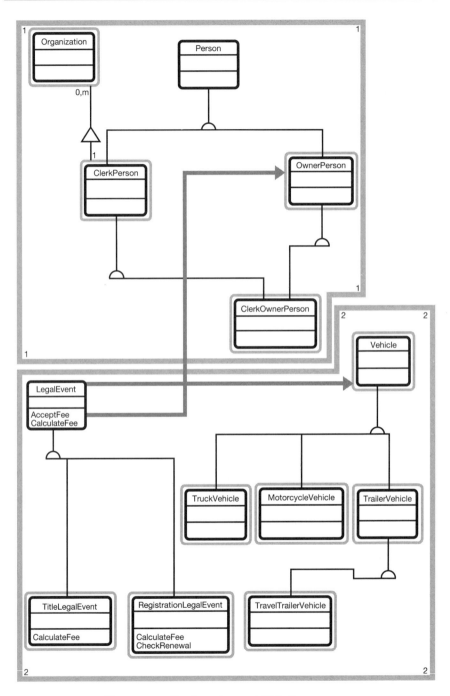

Figure 7.23: Registration and Title System—
Subject, Class-&-Object, Structure, and Service layers

EXAMPLE—Real-Time Airlift System

Note that the majority of the symbols in this Service layer have no explicit Services; they all have the implicit Services (create, connect, access, release), not normally shown on the Service layer.

The SearchAirspace Service searches an airspace for an airborne item; the airborne item could be an aircraft, a hot air balloon, or a flock of birds; all that is known at this point is that something is at a particular position in space at a specific point in time. Once it finds something, SearchAirspace sends an AirborneItem.Create message, to create and initialize (with whole-part) a new AirborneItem Object. Next, AirborneItem.StartTrajectory sends an AirborneItemTrajectory.Create message, to create (and initialize, reflecting a whole-part) a new AirborneItemTrajectory. Each AirborneItemTrajectory has an on-going CalculateTrajectory Service; that Service uses an AirborneItem.Access message in support of its calculations. Manually, a known Aircraft Object and a particular AirborneItemTrajectory Object can be mapped to each other; this is done using the implicit Access Services for Aircraft and AirborneItemTrajectory.

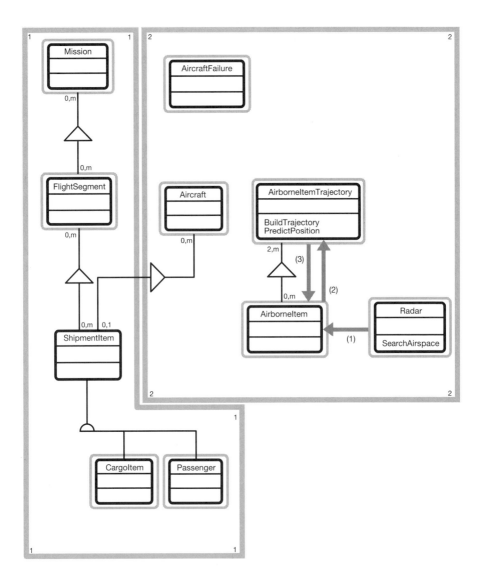

Figure 7.24: Real-Time Airlift System—
Subject, Class-&-Object, Structure, and Service layers

8

Selecting CASE for OOA

8.1 CASE—AND SOME PUZZLING QUESTIONS

Computer-Aided Software Engineering (CASE)—it's hard to believe that such simplistic software tools are getting so much attention these days. The marketeers race to the drawing board, finding new ways to make their CASE product more provocative than the competition's.

Yet is it really CASE? The term "CASE" usually refers to limited graphics and text tools. Perhaps a less sexy but more accurate name would be CADC—Computer-Aided Drawing and Checking. This quieter acronym would go a long way toward controlling your management's expectations of such products.

Why so little for (often) so much—in software cost, training cost, and support cost? Many tools consist of rigid graphics, simple text, rudimentary syntax checks, and a sub-standard human interface, at a surprisingly high price per copy.

Could simple drawing tools and a part-time clerk/diagram-checker be more cost effective? Could such an approach reduce risk—in cost, schedule, and management frustration?

Why are the tools hard-wired to a particular method (i.e., compliant with the DeMarco "Standard" (circa 1978) or the Coad/Yourdon "Standard" (circa 1991))? Why not allow the user to define his project's notations for nodes, connectors, connection rules, and the like—and then use the CASE tool he has defined in data?

Who uses CASE products? Is the human interface so tedious that the engineers pass red-lined documents to a clerk, to feed in the data? (If so, are only clerk copies needed?) Does the vendor sell a course just to teach someone how to use his product? (If so, just how poor is the human interface?)

For organizations that made a purchase, is the product still in use one year later? How much of it? What were the biggest problems? Did they find an automated work-around? Did it become "shelfware"?

8.2 EXPANDING CASE

CASE can be viewed in a much larger context than the hotly publicized tools of the present. One would like to see automated assistance for the *entire* systems development life cycle, which involves over 100 functional capabilities; most commercially available products have a maximum of 20–30 such functional capabilities.[1]

8.3 WHAT'S NEEDED FOR OOA

CASE support for OOA requires the following:

8.3.1 Notation

Notation includes the five layer OOA model, and its symbols—

- Subject layer
  Subject
- Class-&-Object layer
  Class-&-Object
  Class
- Structure layer
  Gen-Spec Structure
  Whole-Part Structure
- Attribute layer
  Attribute
  Instance Connection
- Service layer
  Service
  Message Connection

and the Class-&-Object specification template, which includes—

- Object State Diagram
  State
  Transition
- Service Chart
  Condition
  Text block
  Loop
  Connector

[1] A representative list of CASE functions is discussed in "More on the Future of CASE" [Yourdon, 1988b].

These symbols are summarized in Appendix A, and on the inside book covers of this text.

8.3.2 Layers

Layer support needs to include on/off selection of the five OOA Layers (Subject, Class-&-Object, Structure, Attribute, and Service).

Subjects may be collapsed (identifying only their numbers and names), partially expanded (listing their Class-&-Objects), or fully expanded (showing Subject partitioning boxes, layered along with the other OOA layers).

8.3.3 Advanced Features

One advanced feature is reuse support. This includes searching, browsing, classifying, and extracting previous OOA results.

Another advanced feature helps with depicting the behavior dynamics. Inbound and outbound Message Connections may be highlighted, based upon the selection of a Service or Services. Alternatively, threads of execution can be displayed—one at a time, or all together, using different line patterns for each thread—once they have been defined by the analyst.

8.3.4 Model Checks

Model checks provide early warnings of errors, inconsistencies, and unnecessary complexity.

These checks may be done manually (with a checklist, by a clerk) or with the aid of a CASE tool for OOA. When automated, the checks should be project-definable as warnings (rules that can be broken) or as errors (rules that one is not allowed to violate).

Each Class-&-Object:

* has a name
* has a unique name (within the model)
* has more than 1 Attribute
* has 1 or more Instance Connections
* has 1 or more Message Connections
* has unique Attribute names (within the symbol)
* has unique Service names (within the symbol)

Each Template:

- has a specification of each Attribute
- has a specification of each Service
- has content consistent with the layers
- has a usage of each named input/output within the specification text

Each Gen-Spec Structure:

- has more than 1 Attribute or Service per level
- has 2 to 4 levels (else getting too complex)
- has Attribute names which are unique within ancestors and descendants
- has Attribute and Service names which do not appear across an entire specialization level
- has unique Attribute and Service names in generalizations for each portion of a lattice

8.4 WHAT'S AVAILABLE

We use what we like to call "CardCASE."[2] It seems like a very promising—and extremely inexpensive—tool for object-oriented brainstorming. We use ordinary index cards (commonly called 3" x 5" cards, in the USA) or Post-it™ notes. We write the name of each potential Class-&-Object on a separate card. Then we put the cards on an 11" x 17" inch pad of paper (although a white board with magnets does nicely for larger systems). Index cards are *very* effective tools for OOA. They help us extract problem domain understanding and the system's responsibilities as we interact with our clients.

OOA CASE tools, combined with a large screen projection system, closely approximate the "look and feel" of index cards for team interaction, even in initial model development.

As of this writing, OOA CASE tools include:

- Object-Oriented Environment
  Fuji Xerox Information Systems
  Tokyo, Japan

---

[2] We developed this idea after hearing about Ward Cunningham (Wyatt Software Services, Inc., Lake Oswego, Oregon USA) and his "Class-Responsibilities-Collaborators" (CRC) cards.

- OOA*Tool*™
  Object International, Inc.
  Austin, Texas USA

- ObjectPlus™
  Easyspec, Inc.
  Houston, Texas USA

- Adagen™
  Mark V Systems, Ltd.
  Encino, California USA

Others are in progress.

8.5 ADDITIONAL CONSIDERATIONS

Many additional considerations come into play when evaluating and introducing CASE into a project, e.g., tool connectivity, team support, standards conformance, and reusability support. For this book, we'll stick to the OOA-specific requirements for CASE; however, the ideal OO-CASE tool will allow seamless integration of OOA, OOD, OO-implementation, and OO-testing.

For additional reading, refer to books and publications that focus on such matters, including *CASE Is Software Automation* [McClure, 1989] and *CASE: Using Software Development Tools* [Fisher, 1989].

9
Moving to
Object-Oriented Design

9.1 LOOKING AHEAD TO OOD

This chapter looks ahead to object-oriented design (OOD). For a more comprehensive treatment of OOD itself, please refer to the next volume in this series, *Object-Oriented Design* [Coad and Yourdon, 1991].

9.2 ONE UNDERLYING MESSAGE

For requirements analysts, this chapter drives home one underlying message: moving from OOA to OOD is a progressive expansion of the model. The OOA layers model *the problem domain and the system's responsibilities*. The OOD expansion of the OOA layers model a particular *implementation*. The expansion occurs primarily with added components—human interaction, task management, and data management.

This expansion is in contrast to the radical movement from data flow diagrams to structure charts (or from data flow diagrams to an object-oriented representation). Such movement is abrupt and forever disjoint: designers get a hint from the analysis, and then go off to the "real" design. Such an approach also fails to bring the requirements as a central issue into design. Moreover, meaningful traceability—one which supports the process itself—withers away.

9.3 ANALYSIS VS. DESIGN

OOA identifies and defines Class-&-Objects which directly reflect the problem domain and the system's responsibilities within it.

OOD identifies and defines additional Class-&-Objects, reflecting an implementation of the requirements (Dialogue layer, Task Management layer, Data Management layer). Good design practice implies trade-offs between some number of potential approaches.

So OOA and OOD are distinct disciplines.

These disciplines may be applied in sequence (OOA, then OOD). Such an approach helps with larger teams (different schedules, possibly different teams) and larger problem domains (where analysis may be conducted at a higher level of abstraction).

These disciplines may be intertwined (OOA, then OOD, then some more of each, again and again). In small teams, especially in a prototyping-conducive environment (e.g., Smalltalk), the activities and focus of OOA and OOD are often interleaved.

9.4 MULTI-LAYER, MULTI-COMPONENT MODEL

The Multi-Layer, Multi-Component Model consists of five layers, extended during design using four major components: human interaction, problem domain, task management, and data management.

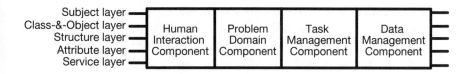

Figure 9.1: Multi-Layer, Multi-Component Model

The Human Interaction Component includes the actual displays and inputs needed for effective human-computer interaction. Example Classes include Window, Pane, and Selector.

OOA results are placed inside the Problem Domain Component. Within this component there is the potential need to manage combinations and splits of certain OOA Class-&-Objects, Structures, Attributes, and Services. Possible reasons include: timing and sizing trade-offs, chunking for storage management, chunking to support assignments to team members, and adjusting to domain-specific Classes which are available for reuse. Example Classes include Clerk, Vehicle, Owner, and LegalEvent (for a motor vehicle registration and title system).

The Task Management Component includes real time task definition, communication, and coordination. It also includes hardware allocation considerations and external system and device protocols. Example Classes include TaskManager and Task.

The Data Management Component includes access and management of persistent data. It isolates the data management concerns—flat file, relational DBMS, or object-oriented DBMS. Example Classes include Parser, ParseTree, and ParseVariable (for a tagged language flat file manager).

9.5 A CONTINUUM OF REPRESENTATION

This section looks at a continuum of representation—using problem-domain constructs all the way through the development process. It also discusses what to do with less than a continuum, and programming language impact.

9.5.1 A Continuum: OOA to OOD to OOI to OOT

Object-orientation uses problem domain constructs to provide a continuum of representation from OOA to OOD to OO-implementation (OOI) to OO-test (OOT) (and then to ongoing engineering, a continuing application of these disciplines).[1]

OOA is programming language-independent. Preliminary OOD remains largely language-independent. Detailed OOD is language-dependent, and can be effectively applied for procedural, package-oriented, and object-oriented programming languages.

Language and data management tools affect how much of the OOA and OOD semantics are captured explicitly in the application code itself—mapped directly into object-oriented programming language (OOPL) syntax and data management syntax.

9.5.2 Less Than a Continuum: What to Do

What if you are caught somewhere in the development activities for a software system?

As an analyst. OOA is programming language-independent. The underlying principles—

---

[1] In contrast, functional approaches drop problem domain understanding "on the cutting room floor" (as they say in the motion picture industry), at the very start of analysis.

- Abstraction
    Procedural
    Data
- Encapsulation
- Inheritance
- Association
- Communication Through Messages
- Pervading Methods of Organization
    Objects and Attributes
    Whole and Parts
    Classes and Members, and distinguishing between them
- Behavior Categories
    Immediate Causation
    Change over Time
    Similarity of Functions

and model notations and strategies for establishing—

- Subject layer
- Class-&-Object layer
- Structure layer
- Attribute layer
- Service layer

all work together to give the analyst effective thinking tools to get his job accomplished. No assumption is made about the design method or the programming language(s) that may be used to build the system.

As a designer. If you receive a non-OOA requirements specification, rapidly develop (say over 1–4 weeks) an OOA model, using the Services specifications to trace back to the functions in the supplied requirements specification. Resolve the holes you'll uncover along the way. Next apply preliminary OOD; then apply detailed OOD, aimed at the programming language(s) to be used for implementation.

As an implementer. If you receive a non-OOD specification, yet you plan on implementing the design using an OOPL, rapidly develop (1–4 weeks) an OOA model, and expand into an OOD model.

Finally, apply detailed OOD, focusing on off-the-shelf Classes and reusability.

Can you apply OOA and OOD, even though your organization mandates (by official policy or corporate culture) that all systems must be coded using fourth-generation languages (4GLs), or COBOL, or both? Yes. As Michael Millikin described it:

> Language battles aside, however, programmers can exploit object-oriented software design concepts even with traditional languages. [Millikin, 1989]

Language selection significantly affects the strategy and focus underlying OOD. Language selection also affects how much predefined syntax is available for expressing OOA and OOD semantics. Yet eventual implementation in a procedural or package-oriented language does not affect the effective use of OOA or OOD.

9.5.3 Programming Language Impact

All languages permit OOI. Yet some languages provide a much richer syntax for explicitly capturing the underlying representation used during OOA and OOD.

As Bjarne Stroustrup pointed out in "What Is Object-Oriented Programming?":

> A language is said to support a style of programming if it provides facilities that makes it convenient (reasonably easy, safe, and efficient) to use that style. [Stroustrup, 1988b]

Let's return to the principles for managing complexity, and examine the syntax support provided by four implementation language categories: procedural programming languages, package-oriented programming languages, object-oriented programming languages, and finally object-oriented database languages.

OOD and Procedural Languages

For procedural languages (e.g., C, Pascal, FORTRAN, 4GLs, and COBOL), only procedural abstraction is directly supported by a language. Data abstraction and encapsulation can be added by style guides, programmer discipline, and team inspection "enforcement." (This discipline is used in practice to some extent already, by designers applying structured design's information-hiding module.) Inheritance cannot be explicitly shown, although some of the commonality can be factored out into individual routines (with very limited possibilities for subsequent reuse). And the pervading methods of organization have no explicit support.

OOD leading to a procedural language is not technically gratifying, perhaps. Yet it does fit into a practical, viable approach: OOA, to OOD, to procedural language with OO conventions. For some of our clients, this approach is exactly what is needed within the organization today (with a view towards introducing OOPLs over time).

Technology transition across an entire discipline seems to take about a generation. Consider the fact that many systems analysts today have not yet heard of something called "structured analysis!" Patience is most desirable.

OOD and Package-Oriented Languages

For package-oriented languages (e.g., Ada), procedural abstraction, data abstraction, encapsulation, and one of the pervading methods of organization (objects and attributes) have direct syntax support. Inheritance cannot be explicitly shown[2,3]; some of the other commonality can be factored out into individual routines (with very limited possibilities for subsequent reuse). Two of the pervading methods of organization (classes and members, and whole and parts) have no explicit representation. OOD leading to a package-oriented language is palatable, perhaps, and it presents a viable development approach: OOA to OOD to package-oriented language with OO conventions. For our military and other real-time government system clients, this approach reflects exactly what will happen for many years to come.[4]

OOD and Object-Oriented Programming Languages

Object-oriented languages (e.g., C++, Smalltalk, Objective-C, Actor, and Eiffel) directly support procedural abstraction (within a method), data abstraction, encapsulation, inheritance, and two of the

---

[2] Yes, genericity (type-independent parameters) is helpful, but it is no substitute for inheritance.

[3] At some point, Ada itself is likely to include Classes, Objects, and inheritance. In the interim, Software Productivity Solutions of Melbourne, Florida markets ClassicAda™, a preprocessor which provides the missing object-oriented constructs.

[4] The big payoff for the government in using a package-oriented language over a procedural language should be during maintenance! The richer syntax provides a means to express more of the design structure explicitly in the code. Automated tools can generate pictures of the design directly from the code; the team can review the picture of the design, knowing that it's up-to-date. In addition, explicit data abstraction makes it harder for a programmer to sneak in a routine to grab some data directly, rather than using Services that exclusively manipulate the data.

three pervading methods of organization (objects and attributes, and classes and members). Assemblies are not explicitly supported, but are conveniently expressed with composite Objects. So OOA to OOD to OOPL is an approach with a very consistent underlying representation.

An OOPL directly supports Message Connections. An OOPL only implicitly supports Whole-Part Structures (using nested Objects, organized by what is referred to as a client-server construct). An OOPL implicitly supports Instance Connections (mappings between Objects).

Using an OOPL, the designer takes on a wholly different design focus. The designer considers a part of the design, and then examines existing Classes that are like or somewhat like that part of the design—meaning, close in their variables and methods. The designer then inherits that capability and extends it with sub-Classes.

OOD and Object-Oriented Database Languages

An Object-Oriented Database Management System (OO-DBMS) and its language are a combination of an OOPL with data management capabilities. But just as not all relational products are really relational, and not all object-oriented products are object-oriented, it's not too surprising that not all OO-DBMSs are necessarily "OO" or "DBMSs."

Four different architectures underlie the OO-DBMS field:

- Big attribute—an RDBMS is extended to allow big data attributes, e.g., a document. Example: the "object-oriented" product from Informix (Lenexa, Kansas USA).

- Loosely coupled—an OOPL and a number of possible DBMSs are combined. Example: *Nexpert Object* from Neuron Data (Palo Alto, California USA), working with a number of commercial RDBMSs.

- Tightly-coupled—an OOPL and a specific data management system are offered as an integrated system. Examples: *GemStone* form Servio Logic (Alameda, California USA); *Ontos* from Ontologic (Billerica, Massachusetts USA).

- Extended relational—an RDBMS is extended to allow data attributes of type "procedure." Example: Relational Technology's *Postgres*.

The tightly coupled architecture, which uses a single language for both programming and data manipulation, seems like the winner in the long run, in its explicit capture of OOA and OOD semantics.

9.6 WRAP UP

OOA tackles the problem domain and the system's responsibilities within it. OOD moves further, adding the details needed for a particular implementation to fulfill those responsibilities. OOA and OOD fit together in a consistent, systematic approach to more effective analysis and design.

10

Getting Started With OOA

This chapter addresses key issues related to introducing OOA into an organization, in four major sections:

- Is OOA the new silver bullet?
- Is this the time to start using OOA?
- Is it revolution or evolution?
- How should we begin?

10.1 IS OOA THE NEW SILVER BULLET?

As the software industry continues to be plagued with problems of low productivity and poor quality, companies around the world are constantly looking for new solutions—in the form of tools, techniques, and methods. Structured techniques were hailed by some as the productivity solution in the 1970 and early 1980s; CASE was unveiled as the productivity solution of the second half of the 1980s; and now some are suggesting that "object orientation" is the salvation for the 1990s. Disturbingly, each new solution is adopted with almost religious fanaticism: in some organizations, structured techniques are now dismissed as the "old religion" of the ancient 1970s and object-oriented techniques are embraced as the "new religion" of the 1990s. Just as *Business Week* magazine proclaimed in a 1988 cover story that CASE tools could "save" American business, now we are seeing popular journals proclaim object-oriented techniques a "revolution."

In a delightful essay entitled "No Silver Bullet" [Brooks, 1988], Fred Brooks argued persuasively that there are no "magic" solutions to the fundamentally difficult problems associated with software development. There are no panaceas, no miracle cures that will automatically increase our productivity by a factor of ten, while simultaneously eliminating all bugs and software defects. Structured techniques, object-oriented techniques, and CASE tools can help—but as several industry pundits have observed, "A fool with a tool is still a fool."

We want to make sure you have no illusions about OOA as a potential "silver bullet." While we have stressed the benefits and advantages of OOA throughout this book, there is no guarantee that object-oriented modeling techniques can prevent a project disaster. An inexperienced analyst who does a poor job of interviewing the user community may not discover all of the relevant objects in the system; an uncooperative and recalcitrant user may fail to describe some of the attributes, services, or instance connections in the system model. And, of course, any project—regardless of the tools and methods it uses—can suffer the problems of politics, mismanagement, and incompetent project personnel.

10.2 IS THIS THE TIME TO START USING OOA?

For many organizations, the issue is not whether OOA will produce miracles, but whether it represents a substantially different approach to systems development that should be adopted as a new standard. As we pointed out in Chapter 1, OOA *is* substantially different than functional decomposition, structured analysis, and typical information modeling methods. But even if it is different and "better" (in some sense of the word) than other methods, is 1990 the best time to start using OOA? Would it be better for the typical organization to wait until 1991? or 1995? or 2000?

To answer this question, it is useful to think of OOA as one aspect of an object-oriented "paradigm" or "technology." (Other aspects might be object-oriented programming, object-oriented design, object-oriented domain analysis, etc.) Most technologies—whether hardware-oriented or software-oriented, computer-related or non-computer-related—follow an evolutionary curve suggested by Figure 10.1.

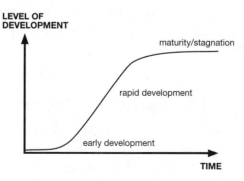

Figure 10.1: Technology evolution

Thus, one could argue that the "structured revolution" began in the late 1960s with the introduction of structured programming; it advanced rapidly through the 1970s and early 1980s with the development of structured design and structured analysis. In the mid-1980s, some additional refinements were added for real-time systems (e.g., the introduction of state-transition diagrams, and control flows in data flow diagrams), and a modeling technique known as "event partitioning" was substituted in place of the "pure" top-down decomposition of data flow diagrams. But since 1986, virtually nothing has happened to the technology of structured techniques; CASE tools have provided automated support, but the underlying paradigm remains the same.

From this perspective, OOA and the related object-oriented techniques represent a *new* technology curve; whether we are currently in the "early development" phase or the "rapid development" phase is a matter of debate, but there is little question that object-oriented methods are fundamentally different than the traditional methods currently being used by most organizations.

As a result, the real question that a typical organization has to address is: is this the best time to "jump" off one technology curve and onto another? We believe there are four major issues involved in this decision:

- Is the object-oriented paradigm sufficiently mature and well-developed?
- Is there a good object-oriented implementation technology available? Does the organization provide adequate tools for its practitioners to effectively use object-oriented techniques?
- Is the organization sophisticated enough to successfully change its development methods?
- Are the systems and applications being developed by the organization the kind that will most effectively use the object-oriented paradigm?

Each of these issues is explored in the sections which follow.

10.2.1 Is the Object-Oriented Paradigm Mature?

Some practitioners argue that object-oriented methods are still new and somewhat immature; consequently, they are unwilling to risk their company's involvement in the methods until they evolve further. Indeed, when we wrote the first edition of this book in early 1989, we felt much the same way; this new edition is a reflection of the changes and refinements that we have made based on considerable teaching and consulting experience during the course of a year. The relative immaturity of object-oriented analysis and design may also be judged by the paucity of books, training courses, and CASE tools.

On the other hand, object-oriented *programming* is a fairly well-developed technology; such languages have been around since the late 1960's; today, a plethora of books, training courses, videotapes, and programming languages support this approach.

Each organization will have to decide for itself when the family of object-oriented technologies is sufficiently mature to justify pilot-project experimentation or full-fledged support. Obviously, this will also involve the organization's choice to be a "leading-edge" technology-oriented organization, or a more conservative organization that waits until new technologies are well established.

10.2.2 Is There a Good Object-Oriented Implementation Technology?

As we pointed out in Chapter 9, object-oriented design and implementation can be carried out in a "traditional" software environment, using classical third-generation programming languages. Realistically, though, many organizations may postpone their commitment to object-oriented techniques until they see a clear path from object-oriented analysis through object-oriented design and directly into an object-oriented programming language.

Consequently, it is fairly common to see organizations adopting object-oriented techniques if they are using a package-oriented language (like Ada) or an object-oriented language (like Smalltalk, C++, or Eiffel). On the other hand, it is relatively uncommon, as this second edition is being written, to see business data processing organizations adopting object-oriented analysis and design—simply because it is less obvious how it will work in COBOL; yet even among these organizations, leading edge business data processing firms have already embraced OOA and OOD, expecting a gradual transition into object-oriented languages as they become available in a dialect with which they are more comfortable.

In late 1989, the CODASYL standards organization created a new subcommittee to recommend changes to the COBOL language to "make COBOL object-oriented." Though the next official version of COBOL is not scheduled to be released until 1999 (!), we feel it is highly likely that one or more compiler vendors will release interim versions of object-oriented COBOL (which perhaps could be called COBOL++ or Objective-COBOL!) by 1991 or 1992. And this development may dramatically speed up the adoption of object-oriented techniques within the business data processing community.

10.2.3 Is the Organization Sophisticated Enough?

Recently, a great deal of attention has been focused on "process models." Based largely on the work of Watts Humphrey and his colleagues at the Software Engineering Institute, there is a growing consensus that organizations can exist at any one of five levels of "process maturity" [Humphrey, 1989]. In summary form, the five levels he describes are as follows:

- *Initial* level (level 1). There is no formal method, no consistency, no standards on how systems should be built. Each software developer considers himself an artist; anarchy prevails.

- *Repeatable* level (level 2). There is a consensus within the organization about "the way we do things around here," but it has not been formalized or written down. The systems development process is statistically stable through rigorous management of costs and schedules, but success depends on the individual skills of project managers; the process has not been "institutionalized."

- *Managed* level (level 3). There is a formal, documented process for developing systems. Software inspections are rigorous, and configuration management is more advanced than at level 2. There is a "software process group" that constantly refines and updates the organization's methods.

- *Measured* level (level 4). The organization has instituted formal process measurements—often referred to as "software metrics"—to measure its *process* for building systems, as well as the resulting *products*.

- *Optimized* level (level 5). The organization uses the measurements from level 4 as a feedback mechanism to improve those parts of its process that are found to be weak or deficient.

There is general agreement that an organization cannot make effective use of new tools (e.g., CASE tools) or methods (e.g., OOA) unless it is at level 3. While this may seem like common sense, the sobering fact is that approximately 85% of large U.S. organizations surveyed in the late 1980s were found to be at level 1; another 10–12% were at level 2; and only about 3% were at level 3. As of mid-1990, no organizations had been found at level 4 or level 5 in the U.S.

10.2.4 Is the Organization Building Systems that Will Exploit Object-Oriented Techniques?

One of the characteristics of a paradigm shift is that people (and organizations) generally adopt a new technology simply to solve familiar problems more quickly or efficiently. Because of the cost of making the shift (e.g., training costs) and the natural inertia of the human animal (as well as the conservative nature of the organizations to which we belong), it is likely that people will continue using older technologies until "order-of-magnitude" improvements are available, *or until new problems appear which cannot practicably be solved with older technologies.*

A case in point: software managers at IBM commented to the authors that all of their attempts to use standard structured techniques to build applications in the OS/2-EE Presentation Manager environment have been dismal failures; the only successes they could point to were applications developed with object-oriented techniques.

The OS/2-EE Presentation Manager environment is typical of what many call the "GUI environment" today: a graphical user interface, characterized by pull-down menus, multiple windows, icons rather than textual commands, and mouse-driven commands. In such an environment, the new object-oriented paradigm excels; the older structured approach typically fails.

But it must be remembered that not everyone is building systems in a GUI environment. Many organizations are still using dumb terminals with character-based input commands, or building batch systems with card input and magnetic tape output. Walking into some shops is like walking through a time warp and watching the calendar turn back to 1968.

If you are spending your days developing batch payroll systems that are fundamentally the same as the payroll systems of the 1960s and 1970s, and if your only desire is to improve productivity by 10%, it will be hard to justify a major transition to object-oriented systems development techniques. But if you are building new systems for which the conventional technologies are demonstrably inadequate, then it may be appropriate to begin using object-oriented techniques.

10.3 REVOLUTION VERSUS EVOLUTION

As we mentioned earlier, many discussions of object-oriented techniques degenerate into fervent debates about good versus bad and the relative merits of "new" and "old" methods.

In many of these discussions, OOA and OOD are portrayed as "revolutions" which can (and should) completely replace the earlier structured techniques. The furthest fringe of the object-oriented camp even goes so far as to suggest that all of the software developed with earlier methods is no good, and should be thrown out; and that the earlier generation of software engineers (those now in their 40s), who were weaned on structured techniques, are unsalvageable and should be put out to pasture.

Another group, which we label the "synthesists," argues that object-oriented techniques and structured techniques are compatible, and that many of the best ideas of both techniques can be used together. As an example, some of the synthesists point out that the event-partitioning approach of structured analysis can be carried out in such a way as to identify a number of discrete bubbles (functions) which surround local data stores in a data flow diagram. Grouping the bubbles and the data store together is, according to this group, essentially the same as creating objects; thus, *voilà!*, the system model produced by structured analysis has been "objectified."

We have no doubt that one could arrive at the same result using different methods; but it has also been our experience that the thinking process, the discovery process, and the communication between user and analyst are fundamentally different with OOA than with structured analysis. Thinking about objects is fundamentally different than thinking about functions. In that regard, we side squarely with the revolutionaries, though we disagree with the proposition that older software engineers who began with structured techniques are incapable of shifting to the new object-oriented view of the world.

At the same time, we agree with the fundamental message of the synthesists, even though we disagree with many of their examples and tactics. Fundamental concepts such as abstraction, partitioning, conscious deferral of design decisions, etc. are just as relevant in OOA as they were in the days of structured analysis. When structured design was first developed, one of the fundamental concepts was that of "design evaluation criteria": guidelines and heuristics that one could use to distinguish between good designs and bad designs. Now, as the authors begin extending OOA into OOD, we find that there is also a set of evaluation criteria to help us distinguish between good object-oriented designs and bad ones.

10.4 HOW SHOULD WE BEGIN?

Getting started with OOA is, in many ways, the same as getting started with any new technology or method. You must first perceive that there is a problem that OOA can solve, and that your conventional approach won't solve adequately. Then you must "sell" the OOA concept to others in the organization: senior managers who must invest money and provide support; middle-level managers who must figure out how to use a new technology without disrupting their schedules and budgets; and various levels of technicians who may or may not be enthusiastic about adopting new techniques. Pilot projects are a necessity with OOA, as with any other new technology, in order to gain experience and adapt the method to local needs. Training is inevitably required, and a careful implementation plan must be laid out.

Since the details of getting started with OOA (e.g., what kind of pilot project should we choose? How long will the training take? etc.) are so similar to those for other new computer technologies, it makes sense to take advantage of the "technology transfer" strategies that people have already developed. For additional reading, consult *Agents of Change* [Bouldin, 1989] and *Managing the Structured Techniques* [Yourdon, 1988a].

10.5 CONCLUSION

We are obviously enthusiastic about the future of object-oriented techniques, and OOA in particular. While acknowledging the importance and relevance of many earlier methods, we have now left them behind; neither author has drawn a single data flow diagram in the past few years, except (on rare occasions) as a way of partitioning complex Services in an OOA model. For us, OOA is the future, and the future is here and now.

However, we recognize that large organizations change slowly; old methods and habits are hard to change, and old software may last for decades before it can be replaced with new software developed with new methods. Consequently, we see the 1990s as a period of gradual acceptance of OOA.

We are dedicated to continue applying and advancing this method in practice. We look forward to hearing from you, and working together with you, in applying OOA.

Appendix A

Summary of Notations & Strategies

This chapter presents a concise summary of OOA notations and strategies. It concludes with an OOA model of OOA itself.

A.1 OOA NOTATIONS

OOA notations are summarized on pages 196 and 197.

A.2 OOA STRATEGIES

This section presents strategy summaries. It's terse, to the point, and useful once you have studied Chapters 3–7.

OOA strategies are summarized on pages 198 through 204.

A.3 AN OOA MODEL OF OOA ITSELF

Figure A.5 presents another way to summarize OOA notation, using OOA notation to describe OOA itself.

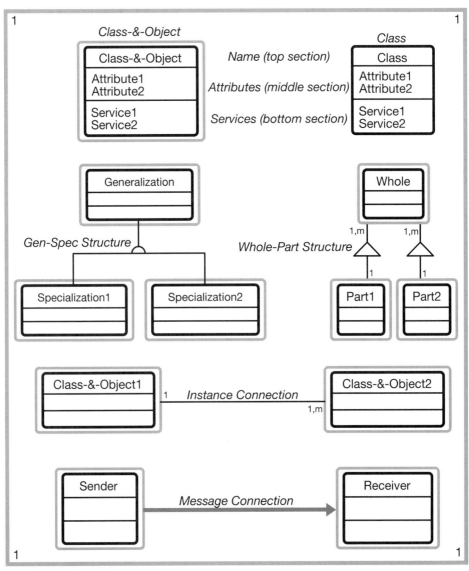

Subject (may be expanded or collapsed)

Note: In addition, OOA uses Object State Diagrams and Service Charts for specifying Services.

Figure A.1: OOA notations

specification
  attribute
  attribute
  attribute

  externalInput
  externalOutput

  objectStateDiagram

  additionalConstraints

  notes

  service <name & Service Chart>
  service <name & Service Chart>
  service <name & Service Chart>

and, as needed,
  traceabilityCodes
  applicableStateCodes
  timeRequirements
  memoryRequirements

Figure A.2: Class-&-Object specification template

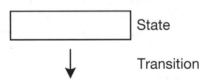

State

Transition

Figure A.3: Object State Diagram notation (used within the template)

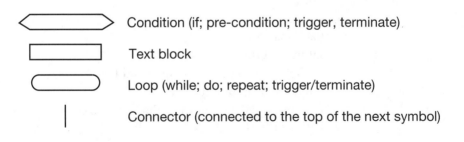

Condition (if; pre-condition; trigger, terminate)

Text block

Loop (while; do; repeat; trigger/terminate)

Connector (connected to the top of the next symbol)

Figure A.4: Service Chart notation (used within the template, for each Service)

STRATEGY—Finding Class-&-Objects

Object. An abstraction of something in a problem domain, reflecting the capabilities of a system to keep information about or interact with it; an encapsulation of Attribute values and their exclusive Services.

Class. A description of one or more Objects with a uniform set of Attributes and Services, including a description of how to create new objects in the Class.

Class-&-Object. A term meaning "a Class and the Objects in that Class."

How to name.

Use a singular noun or adjective & noun; describe a single Object in the Class; adhere to the standard vocabulary for the problem domain.

Where to look

Observe first-hand; listen actively; check previous OOA results; check other systems; read, read, read; and prototype.

What to look for

Look for structures, other systems, devices, things or events remembered, roles played, operational procedures, sites, and organizational units.

What to consider and challenge

Needed remembrance, needed behavior, (usually) multiple Attributes, (usually) more than one Object in a Class, always applicable Attributes, always-applicable Services, domain based requirements, and not merely derived results.

STRATEGY—Identifying Structures

Structure. Structure is an expression of problem-domain complexity, pertinent to the system's responsibilities. The term "Structure" is used as an overall term, describing both Generalization-Specialization (Gen-Spec) and Whole-Part Structures.

Gen-Spec Structures

Consider each Class as a generalization. For its potential specializations, ask:

Is it in the problem domain?

Is it within the system's responsibilities?

Will there be inheritance?

Will the specializations meet the "what to consider and challenge" criteria for Class-&-Objects?

Also, in a similar fashion, consider each Class as a specialization. For its potential generalizations, ask these same questions.

Check previous OOA results in the same and similar problem domains.

If many specializations are possible, consider the simplest specialization and the most elaborate specialization, and then follow with the various ones in between.

The most common form of Gen-Spec Structure is a Gen-Spec hierarchy.

Yet a lattice may be used to:

Highlight additional specializations

Explicitly capture commonality

Only modestly increase model complexity

If a lattice structure becomes unwieldy, consider reorganizing part of it into a hierarchy, which may be more effective in communicating the problem domain and the system's responsibilities.

Avoid naming conflicts within a lattice. Otherwise, a specialization which inherits with name conflicts must include the conflicting names, and then resolve what is required in the corresponding specification.

Whole-Part Structures

What to look for:

Consider these variations—

Assembly-Parts

Container-Contents

Collection-Members

Check previous OOA results in the same and similar problem domains.

What to consider and challenge:

Consider each Object as a whole. For its potential parts, ask:

Is it in the problem domain?

Is it within the system's responsibilities?

Does it capture just a status value? If so, then just include a corresponding Attribute within the whole.

Does it provide a useful abstraction in dealing with the problem domain?

Also, in a similar fashion, consider each Object as a part. For each potential whole, ask these same questions.

Multiple Structures

Multiple Structures sometimes touch top-to-bottom; Instance Connections may map them, side-by-side.

STRATEGY—Identifying Subjects

Subject. A Subject is a mechanism for guiding a reader (analyst, problem domain expert, manager, client) through a large, complex model. Subjects are also helpful for organizing work packages on larger projects, based upon initial OOA investigations.

How to select

Promote the uppermost Class in each Structure upwards to a Subject. Then, promote each Class-&-Object not in a Structure upwards to a Subject. Check previous OOA results in the same and similar problem domains.

How to refine

Refine Subjects by using problem sub-domains. Refine Subjects by using minimal interdependencies (Structures, Instance Connections) and minimal interactions (Message Connections) between them; use the Structure, Attribute, and Service layers to guide you.

How to construct

On the Subject layer, draw each Subject as a simple rectangular box, with a Subject name and number inside. Optionally, list the Classes which are included in the Subject, too.

On other layers, indicate the Subjects with labeled Subject partitioning boxes, to guide the reader from Subject to Subject.

For a large model, as needed to facilitate communication, consider using a separate set of layers for each Subject.

Subjects may be thought of as collapsed, partially expanded (listing its Classes-&-Objects), and fully expanded (Subject partitioning boxes, layered on top of other OOA layers).

A Class-&-Object may be in more than one Subject (when useful in guiding the reader).

Subjects may contain other Subjects, providing multi-level map to guide a reader through a large model.

When to Add

Add once an overall map is needed to guide the various readers through the model.

STRATEGY—Defining Attributes

Attribute. An Attribute is some data (state information) for which each
Object in a Class has its own value.
Identify the Attributes
Questions to ask.
"How am I described in general?"
"How am I described in this problem domain?"
"How am I described in the context of this system's
responsbilities?"
"What do I need to know?"
"What state information do I need to remember over
time?"
"What states can I be in?"
Check previous OOA results in the same and similar problem
domains.
Make each Attribute capture an "atomic concept."
A single value
A tightly-related grouping of values
Whether or not an always-recalculable Attribute is held over
time is a design decision—time vs. memory. Specify the cal-
culation Service, without a corresponding always recalculable
Attribute.
Implicit identifiers, "id" (identifier) and "cid" (connection
identifier), may be used in specification text when needed.
Position the Attributes
Put each Attribute with the Class-&-Object it best describes
(check the problem domain).
Apply inheritance in Gen-Spec Structures
Position the more general Attributes higher.
Position specialized Attributes lower.
Identify Instance Connections
Instance Connection. An Instance Connection is a model of problem
domain mapping(s) that one Object needs with other Objects,
in order to fulfill its responsibilities.
Check previous OOA results in the same and similar problem
domains.
For each Object, add connection lines.
Add subject-matter mappings between Objects,
paying attention to where the connection goes on
Gen-Spec Structures.
For each Object, define the amount or range.

The lower bound
> Optional connection? Lower bound is 0.
> Mandatory connection? Lower bound is 1 or greater.

The upper bound
> Single connection? Upper bound is 1.
> Multiple connections? Upper bound is greater than 1.
> (note: a multiple connection may imply an Attribute to keep track of the current or most recent mapping, e.g., DateTime or Status)

Use the specification template keyword "additional-Constraints" to capture additional constraints, as needed.

Constrain Whole-Part Structures, too. (The difference is the underlying semantic strength.)

Check special cases

Special Cases with Attributes
> Check each Attribute for a value of "not applicable."
> Check each Class-&-Object with just one Attribute.
> Check each Attribute for repeating values.

Special Cases with Instance Connections
> Check each many-to-many Instance Connection.
> Check each Instance Connection between Objects of a single Class.
> Check multiple Instance Connections between Objects.
> Check for additional needed Instance Connections.
> Check for one connecting Object (of many) having special meaning.

Specify the Attributes

Name. (Standard vocabulary. Reflects problem domain, system's responsibilities. Readable. No embedded values.)

Description.

Constraints.
> On constraints
>> May reduce the amount of Service specification needed.
>> Scrutinize cost vs. benefit.
>
> Unit of measure, range, limit, enumeration; default; precision
> Create/access constraint?
> Constrained by other Attributes?
> Traceability code(s), applicable state code(s)
> (option: show such code(s) on the Attribute Layer, for heightened visibility)

STRATEGY—Defining Services

Service. A Service is a specific behavior that an Object is responsible for exhibiting.

Identify Object States

Examine the potential values for the Attributes.

Determine whether the system's responsibilities include different behavior for those potential values.

Check previous OOA results in the same and similar problem domains.

Describe the states and transitions in an Object State Diagram.

Identify the required Services

Algorithmically-simple Services

Create—creates and initializes a new Object in a Class.

Connect—connects (disconnects) an Object with another.

Access—gets or sets the Attribute values of an Object.

Release—releases (disconnects and deletes) an Object.

Algorithmically-complex Services

Check previous OOA results in the same and similar problem domains.

Two categories

Calculate—calculates a result from the Attribute values of an Object.

Monitor—monitors an external system or device. It deals with external system inputs and outputs, or with device data acquisition and control. It may need some companion Services, such as Initialize or Terminate.

Ask

What calculations is the Object responsible for performing on its values?

What monitoring is the Object responsible for doing, in order to detect and respond to a change in an external system or device, i.e., the required event-response behavior?

Use domain-specific names.

Identify Message Connections

Message Connection. A Message Connection models the processing dependency of an Object, indicating a need for Services in order to fulfill its responsibilities.

For each Object—
>What other Objects does it need Services from?
>>Draw an arrow to each of those Objects.
>What other Objects need one of its Services?
>>Draw an arrow from each of those Objects to the one under consideration.
>Follow each Message Connection to the next Object, and repeat the questions.
>Check previous OOA results in the same and similar problem domains.

Examine Message Connection threads.
>Use to check for model completeness (via role-playing simulation, by humans or by computer).
>Use to determine real-time processing requirements (when pertinent)
>"Real time" analysis ⇨ performance requirements
>>Allocate an overall thread budget across the participating Services and Message Connections.

Specify the Services
>Check previous OOA results in the same and similar problem domains.
>Use a template, with an Object State Diagram and Service Charts.
>Use a consistent text block style.
>Express additional constraints.
>Summarize state-dependent Services, using a Services/States table.
>For heightened visibility, consider putting state codes next to the Services on the Service layer itself.

Put the OOA documentation set together
>The Five Layer OOA Model
>The Class-&-Object specifications
>Supplemental documentation, as needed.
>Table of critical threads of execution
>Additional system constraints
>Services/States table

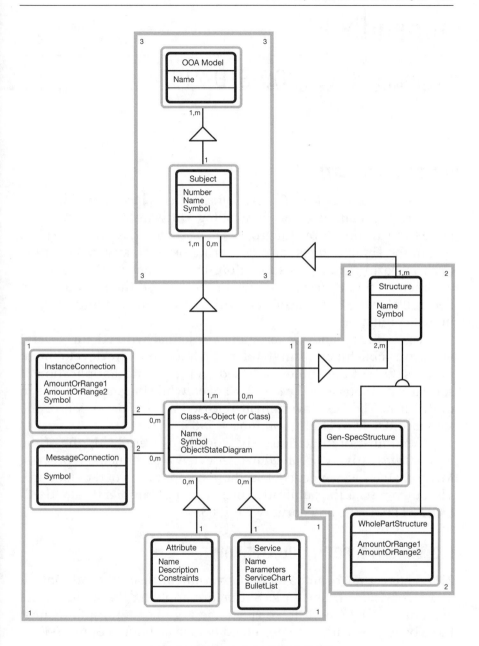

A.5: An OOA model of OOA itself

Appendix B

Mapping OOA to DOD-STD-2167A

B.1 DOD-STD-2167A

DOD-STD-2167A, *Defense System Software Development*, establishes a standard for planning and controlling software development on large software development projects.[1] The standard is primarily used within the United States for engineering-oriented system acquirers (e.g., Department of Transportation, Department of Defense) and contractors. Some countries outside the US use the standard too, generally for work under contract with a US firm developing a system in that country.

US industry and Government personnel worked for several years to establish a uniform standard for large software development projects. One of the authors advised on the practical application of software methods and the standard even while the standard was in draft form. The US Government released an initial version of the standard, DOD-STD-2167, on June 4, 1985.

A number of invitation-only workshops were held; one of the authors was actively involved in this review and refinement process. Many changes were needed, based upon application of the standard. The outcome was the publication of a shorter (!), simpler (!!) standard, DOD-STD-2167A, on February 29, 1988.

B.2 BENEFITS: POINT/COUNTERPOINT

2167A has certain benefits for the Government: visibility and control, and a consistent framework. But before applying the standard, let alone using OOA with it, consider the arguments for and against these benefits—which are presented here in a "point/counterpoint" approach.

[1] *DOD–STD–2167A, Defense System Software Development.* U.S. Department of Defense, February 29, 1988. To request a copy of "2167A" and its Data Item Descriptions, write Naval Publications and Forms Center, 5801 Tabor Ave., Philadelphia, Pennsylvania 19120 USA. (In the U.S., copies may be requested by calling (215) 697-2000.)

Consider the issue of visibility and control. *Point.* The message from the Government to the contractor is simple: cost overruns and schedule setbacks are not acceptable. We want more visibility into what you are doing, and we want you to exert more control over your software development process. Moreover, we want documented systems. *Counterpoint.* Too much time and too much money are the drawbacks. Estimates of the cost of fulfilling 2167A requirements range from 30 to 55 percent of overall cost [Martin, 1988], and talent is consumed fulfilling the letter of the 2167A law. Document-driven engineering (engineering dominated by filling out sections of a document) is all too often weak engineering. Documented systems are vital for helping a maintenance staff understand an overall system during ongoing system maintenance. But, traditionally, no maintainer worth his salt has relied ultimately on anything but the code; even in-line comments are considered suspect by experienced maintainers. Volumes of unread paper won't help reduce the expense of continuing engineering.

Consider instead a consistent framework. *Point.* 2167A provides a consistent framework for software development. Such a framework makes it easier for us to assess progress on the many contracts we are responsible for. And such consistency will eventually help us develop project-level metrics, so we improve the planning and controlling of future projects. *Counterpoint.* Consistency, perhaps, but at what expense—taxpayer dollars for river rafts of documentation? And who is the audience of a five-foot stack of requirements specifications (to use just one example)? The technical staff? No—documents are shipped unread by the technical director (it's simply too much paper). The Government reviewer? No—many times the reviewer's job is to find a maximum number of defects in a very limited time (e.g., 2–4 weeks). So reviewers focus on format and inter-book consistency (referred to as a Sesame Street check: "one of these things is not like the other, one of these things is not the same") rather than on content. A better alternative is a consistent framework applied to a high-level 100-page summary, with a package of engineering products for those few reviewers who have the time and desire to examine the details further.

So, visibility and control, and a consistent framework, are desirable. But to actually achieve these ends takes much more than cranking through a project following the letter of the 2167A law. It takes conscientious, continual effort by both the Government and the contractor to ensure that useful, readable, and read documentation is produced; the documents must be streamlined and focused at specific readers to achieve specific results.

B.3 KEY IMPROVEMENTS WITH 2167A

Two additional 2167A benefits are actually improvements over the earlier 2167 standard. These benefits are development cycle independence and software method independence.

B.3.1 Development Cycle Independence

The earlier 2167 standard presented the classical "waterfall" model for the development cycle—analysis, preliminary design, detailed design, code and unit test, and so forth. 2167 strongly reflected this phase-by-phase approach to software development. Because most Government systems to date had followed that pattern, it seemed reasonable to capture the state of the practice. In contrast, 2167A goes to great pains to avoid even suggesting a development cycle. Rather than use the term "phase" (smacking of a waterfall approach), 2167A uses the term "activity." The contractor defines how to organize activities over time, and includes the description in the Software Development Plan. This lack of Government direction means that the contractor can select his process model—waterfall, rapid prototype, multiple build, spiral, or some hybrid of these. Of course, the selection must be agreed upon by the Government. Once approved, the software development process is established for that contract (modifiable only through agreed-upon revisions to the Software Development Plan).

B.3.2 Software Method Independence

2167 attempted to remain "method independent" and at the same time prescribe some "default methods" that reflected the state of the practice. In applying the standard, the Government and contractor stuck with the default—it seemed the safe thing to do. Yet this default was not the intent of the standard. 2167A again goes to great lengths to avoid suggesting a default or what might be a minimum state of the practice requirement. For example, the major sections of a Software Requirements Specification are no longer broken up into "Functions" (implying a functional decomposition is required), but rather into "Capabilities." The contractor defines what constitutes a capability (e.g., for OOA a Capability may be a Class-&-Object, or a grouping of Class-&-Objects) and includes it in the Software Development Plan. This level of independence means that the contractor can select his software methods (e.g., OOA or some in-house version of OOA for requirements analysis). Yes, the selection must be agreed upon by the Government. And yes, once approved, the software development process is established for that contract (modifiable only through agreed-upon revisions to the Software Development Plan).

These two—development cycle independence and software method independence—are welcome improvements to the standard.

B.4 2167A FOR COMMERCIAL SYSTEMS?

The simple answer to this question is *not a chance*. Visibility and control, and the concept of a consistent framework, can be achieved with simpler standards and lower cost.

Yes, 2167A can be consulted to see what content might be appropriate in your organization. Just remember to consider the costs and benefits every step along the way. And consider how much of your development dollar you are willing to spend on documents. Be sure it is money well spent.

B.5 OOA AND 2167A DOCUMENTATION: AN OVERVIEW

OOA is directly applicable during the system engineering and software requirements analysis activities of 2167A. The remainder of this chapter presents documents of interest in the application of OOA:

For the system engineer:

System/Segment Specification.
System/Segment Design Document.

For software engineering management:

Software Development Plan.

For the software requirements engineer:

Software Requirements Specification(s).
Interface Requirements Specification.

B.6 SYSTEM/SEGMENT SPECIFICATION (SSS)

The System/Segment Specification (SSS) describes the requirements of a system or a segment of a system.
The SSS outline is:

1	**Scope.**
2	**Applicable Documents.**
3	**System Requirements.**
4	**Quality Assurance Provisions.**
5	**Preparation for Delivery.**
6	**Notes.**
10, 20, ...	**Appendixes.**

System engineers can apply OOA to develop engineering results for the paragraphs presented in the following:

3.1   Definition.

This paragraph provides a brief description of the system. So include a "system diagram" (referred to in this document's Data Item Description) and a Subject layer, along with text to give a succinct overview of the system.

Map the results from OOA into this section. Use the Class-&-Object specifications: service requirements; service parameters; pre-conditions, triggers, and terminates; and Object State Diagrams.

Tables can be especially helpful in presenting this state-mode-capability summary.

3.2.1   Performance Characteristics.
3.2.1.X   (State Name).
3.2.1.X.Y   (Mode Name).
3.2.1.X.Y.Z (System Capability Name and Project-Unique Identifier).

This paragraph specifies a capability, its purpose, and its parameters.

3.2.2   System Capability Relationships.
3.2.3   External Interface Requirements.
3.2.3.X   (System Name) External Interface Description.

This paragraph describes the requirements for interfaces with other systems. Detailed interface descriptions are defined in referenced documents.

For each Class-&-Object that corresponds to an external system, include the external inputs and outputs from its Class-&-Object specification.

B.7 SYSTEM/SEGMENT DESIGN DOCUMENT (SSDD)

The System/Segment Design Document (SSDD) specifies the design of a system/segment and its operational and support environments. The SSDD outline is:

1	Scope.
2	Applicable Documents.
3	Operational Concepts.
4	System Design.
5	Processing Resources.
6	Quality Factor Compliance.
7	Requirements Traceability.
8	Notes.
10, 20, ...	Appendixes.

System engineers can apply OOA to develop engineering results for the paragraphs presented in the following:

3.4   System Architecture.

This paragraph describes the internal structure of the system, in terms of segments (sub-systems), Hardware Configuration Items (HWCIs), and Computer Software Configuration Items (CSCIs). It identifies the purpose of and the relationships between components. It also identifies and gives the purpose of external interfaces (external to the system). A "system architecture diagram" (referred to in this document's Data Item Description) may be included.

CSCI selection can have a very significant impact on software development cost.

n CSCIs ⇨

  n Software Requirements Specifications
  n Software Design Documents (Preliminary Design)
  n Software Design Documents (Detailed Design)
  n Software Test Documents

A CSCI is an arbitrary chunk of software used for configuration management and control.

As a requirements engineer, take these factors into consideration when choosing CSCIs:

1. Don't pattern the CSCIs after the hardware architecture.
2. Check the tools and procedures for multi-volume documentation development and production.
3. Identify CSCIs in such a way that Class-&-Objects are not duplicated or split into different CSCIs.

First, a CSCI should not be a reflection of the HWCI architecture. Hardware engineers often seem to think this idea is good; fight them! One reason to avoid using the architecture is its extreme volatility; someday the architecture that was promised to "never, ever, ever change" *will* change, at a disastrous documentation cost. Also, using hardware architecture ignores the fact that more than one piece of hardware may have common software requirements, or ones that are very similar.

Second, consider the question of tools. 2167A book production often involves a good deal of "boiler plate" text. Sections 1 and 2 and the higher-level components of other sections tend to drone on. Do you have the documentation tools and procedures to facilitate writing and maintaining a single copy of such material? And do the tools support inter-book consistency checking or just intra-book consistency checking?

If you don't have the support you need, compare the cost of a single or a few CSCIs to the cost of several dozen. Keep the number of CSCIs down; one CSCI may be quite appropriate.

Third, when multiple CSCIs are desired, select the CSCIs based upon groupings of Subjects, Structures, and Class-&-Objects. Your motivation for this choice is to minimize the interfaces between CSCI volumes, and eliminate requirements redundancy across volumes.

3.5   Operational Scenarios.

This paragraph describes each operational scenario of the system. It identifies the Configuration Items (HWCIs and CSCIs) applicable by states and modes. It also presents the general flow of execution control and data between Configuration Items.

Use OOA to complete this section for the CSCIs you selected. Identify the operational scenarios. Then use the Class-&-Object specifications to identify the state and mode applicability of the CSCIs you chose.

Use Message Connections between Subjects, Structures, and Class-&-Objects in different CSCIs to identify and present the general flow of execution control and data between Configuration Items. Use a state transition diagram to show the overall sequence dependencies between the selected CSCIs.

4	**System Design.**
4.1	**HWCI Identification.**
4.1.X	**(HWCI Name and Project-Unique Identifier).**
4.2	**CSCI Identification.**
4.2.X	**(CSCI Name and Project-Unique Identifier).**

This section identifies the HWCIs and CSCIs. For each CSCI, the section includes a statement of purpose, SSS requirements allocation, interfaces external to the system, interfaces internal to the system, and any design constraints.

Use Message Connections between Subjects, Structures, and Class-&-Objects in different CSCIs to identify the interfaces.

4.4	**Internal Interfaces.**
4.4.1	**(HWCI-to-HWCI).**
4.4.2	**(HWCI-to-CSCI).**
4.4.3	**(CSCI-to-CSCI).**

This section depicts the interfaces internal to the system, showing the interfaces between the Configuration Items (HWCIs and CSCIs), including sender, receiver, and message content.

Again, use Message Connections between Subjects, Structures, and Class-&-Objects in different CSCIs, this time to identify the sender, receiver, and message content.

B.8 SOFTWARE DEVELOPMENT PLAN (SDP)

The Software Development Plan (SDP) describes the contractor's plans for conducting software development.

Keep the SDP at a high level. Use other documents to detail each section. This keeps the SDP less susceptible to change, and keeps the volume from becoming so large as to overwhelm the reader.

The SDP outline is:

1	**Scope.**
2	**Referenced Documents.**
3	**Software Development Management.**

4	**Software Engineering.**
5	**Formal Qualification Testing.**
6	**Software Product Evaluations.**
7	**Software Configuration Management.**
8	**Other Software Development Functions.**
9	**Notes.**
10, 20, ...	**Appendixes.**

Include OOA in the following sections:

3.2	**Schedules and Milestones.**
3.2.1	**Activities.**
3.2.2	**Activity Network.**

These paragraphs briefly describe (in 3.2.1) the software development activities and corresponding schedule. The activity network (3.2.2) shows the sequential constraints among activities. Include the application of OOA in the schedule, with key milestones for versions of the OOA model (e.g., preliminary, draft, and final) and for versions of the Software Requirements Specification(s) and the Interface Requirements Specification.

4.1.3   Software Engineering Environment.

This section includes plans for establishing and maintaining the needed software engineering environment.

Include the hardware and software considerations for CASE tool support of OOA, and support for document generation and production.

4.2.1   Software Development Techniques and Methodologies.

This paragraph identifies and describes the methods to be used for each software development activity.[2]

Identify and briefly describe the use of OOA during the Software Requirements Analysis activity. Also, state that each SRS Capability corresponds to a Class-&-Object or a grouping of Class-&-Objects.

6.5   Activity-Dependent Product Evaluations.

6.5.X   Software Product Evaluation—(activity name).

This paragraph presents plans for conducting project evaluations. Evaluation criteria, procedures, and tools are identified.

---

[2]Methodology is a study of methods. What this paragraph is asking for is methods. Just don't change the 2167A title of this paragraph—your document may be found to be noncompliant if you do!

Include the OOA checklist for early detection and correction of errors, inconsistencies, and unnecessary complexity. Keep the information at a high level; place the detailed checks into a practitioner's notation and strategy sheet.

B.9 SOFTWARE REQUIREMENTS SPECIFICATION (SRS)

The Software Requirements Specification (SRS) specifies the engineering and qualification requirements for a Computer Software Configuration Item (CSCI). The SRS is used as the basis for design and formal testing of a CSCI.

The SRS outline is:

1	Scope.
2	Applicable Documents.
3	Engineering Requirements.
4	Qualification Requirements.
5	Preparation for Delivery.
6	Notes.
10, 20, ….	Appendixes.

Include OOA in the following sections:

3.1   CSCI External Interface Requirements.

This paragraph identifies and describes all interfaces external to the CSCI (meaning with other CSCIs, with HWCIs, and with other systems).

Include the external inputs and outputs from Class-&-Object specifications, and the message interaction between users and the system. Also, include the Message Connections between CSCIs when more than one CSCI is identified in the SSDD.

3.2   CSCI Capability Requirements.

3.2.X   (Capability Name and Project-Unique Identifier).

These paragraphs specify the capability requirements that the CSCI must satisfy. For 3.2, each capability and its states and modes must be summarized.

For 3.2.X, include an OOA diagram fragment for the Subject, Structure, or Class-&-Object(s) to be specified. Then include the corresponding Services specification from the Class-&-Object specifications.

3.3   **CSCI Internal Interfaces.**

This paragraph identifies the interfaces between the capabilities. Include the Message Connections between the capabilities.

3.4   **CSCI Data Element Requirements.**

This paragraph specifies the data elements for the CSCI (both the ones used in its external interfaces and the ones used internally).

Include the Attributes and external inputs and outputs from the Class-&-Object specifications—those which correspond to this CSCI. Be sure to include the required data constraints.

3.5   **Adaptation Requirements.**

3.5.1   **Installation-Dependent Data.**

3.5.2   **Operational Parameters.**

These paragraphs specify the requirements for adapting the CSCI to site-unique conditions and to changes in the environment. In 3.5.1, include the Attributes from "Site" Class-&-Object(s). In 3.5.2, include the Attribute ranges which can be set according to operational need.

3.9   **Design Constraints.**

This paragraph specifies requirements that constrain the CSCI design. Check the design notes folder that you compiled while building the OOA model. If a design constraint really must be levied from within the SRS, do it here.

B.10 INTERFACE REQUIREMENTS SPECIFICATION (IRS)

The Interface Requirements Specification (IRS) specifies the requirements for interfaces between CSCI(s) and other configuration or critical items.

The IRS outline is:

1	Scope.
2	Applicable Documents.
3	Interface Specification.
4	Quality Assurance.
5	Preparation for Delivery.
6	Notes.
10, 20, ….	Appendixes.

Include OOA results in the following paragraphs:

3.1	**Interface Diagrams.**
3.X	**(Interface Name and Project-Unique Identifier).**
3.X.1	**Interface Requirements.**
3.X.2	**Data Requirements.**

This section identifies the interfaces among CSCIs, HWCIs, and critical items to which the specification applies.

Include a "block diagram" (referred to by this document's Data Item Description) depicting the interfaces.

Include the external inputs and outputs from the OOA Class-&-Object specifications, and the message interaction between the user and the system. Also, include the Message Connections between CSCIs when more than one CSCI is identified in the SSDD.

B.11 SUMMARY

You *can* follow good principles of analysis and design, and then figure out how to fit your results into the 2167A framework. Guard against letting the paperwork drive (and potentially overrun) the needed engineering achievements.

Bibliography

OVERVIEW

This bibliography identifies books and articles which have had major impact ("primary bibliography") or some impact ("secondary bibliography") on the development of OOA.

An additional section lists helpful reference publications.

A final section lists related publications by the authors.

PRIMARY BIBLIOGRAPHY

1. Books

[Cherry, 1990] Cherry, George, *Software Construction by Object-Oriented Pictures*. Dorset House, 1990.

[Cox, 1986] Cox, Brad, *Object-Oriented Programming*. Addison-Wesley, 1986.

[Digitalk, 1988] *Smalltalk/V Tutorial and Handbook*. Digitalk, Inc., 1988.

[Meyer, 1988] Meyer, Bertrand, *Object-Oriented Software Construction*. Prentice Hall, 1988.

[Parsaye, Chignell, Khoshafian, and Wong, 1989] Parsaye, Kamran; Chignell, Mark; Khoshafian, Setrag; and Wong, Harry, *Intelligent Databases*. Wiley, 1989.

[Shlaer and Mellor, 1988] Shlaer, Sally and Mellor, Steve, *Object-Oriented Systems Analysis*. Prentice Hall, 1988.

[Tracz, 1988a] Tracz, Will, *Tutorial: Software Reuse: Emerging Technology*. IEEE, 1988.

2. Articles

[Blaha, Premerlani, and Rumbaugh, 1988] Blaha, Michael; Premerlani, William; and Rumbaugh, James, "Relational Database Design Using An Object-Oriented Methodology," *Communications of the ACM*, April 1988.

[Danforth and Tomlinson, 1988] Danforth, Scott and Tomlinson, Chris, "Type Theories and Object-Oriented Programming," *ACM Computing Surveys*, March 1988.

[Hull and King, 1987] Hull, Richard and King, Roger, "Semantic Database Modeling: Survey, Applications, and Research Issues," *ACM Computing Surveys*, September 1987.

[Kang, 1987] Kang, Kyo, "Reuse-Based Development Methodology," *Proceedings from the Workshop on Software Reusability and Maintainability*. National Institute of Software Quality and Productivity, 1987. Also in Tracz, 1988a.

[Ladden, 1989] Ladden, Richard, "A Survey of Issues to be Considered in the Development of an Object-Oriented Development Methodology for Ada," *Ada Letters*, March/April 1989.

[LBMS, 1987] "Entity Life Histories," Learmonth Burchett Management Systems, Houston and London, 1987.

[Loomis, Shaw, and Rumbaugh, 1987] Loomis, M.; Shah, A.; and Rumbaugh, J., "An Object Modeling Technique for Conceptual Design," *European Conference on OOP*, June 1987.

[Lubars, 1988] Lubars, Mitchell, "Code Reusability in the Large versus Code Reusability in the Small," *Tutorial: Software Reuse: Emerging Technology*. IEEE, 1988.

[Prieto-Dias, 1987] Prieto-Dias, Ruben, "Domain Analysis for Reusability," *Proceedings of COMPSAC '87*. IEEE, 1987. Also in Tracz, 1988a.

[Rumbaugh, 1987] Rumbaugh, James, "Relations as Semantic Constructs in an Object-Oriented Language," *ACM OOPSLA '87 Proceedings*, October 1987.

[Seidewitz and Stark, 1987] Seidewitz, Ed and Stark, Mike, "Towards a General Object-Oriented Software Development Methodology," *Ada Letters*, Volume 7, Number 4.

[Stankovic, 1988] Stankovic, John, "Misconceptions About Real-Time Computing," *IEEE Computer*, October 1988.

[Teorey, Yang, and Fry, 1986] Teorey, T.; Yang, D.; and Fry, J., "A Logical Design Methodology for Relational Databases Using the Extended Entity-Relationship Model," *ACM Computing Surveys*, June 1986.

[Thomas, 1989] Thomas, Dave, "What's an Object?", *Byte*, March 1989.

[Tracz, 1988b] Tracz, Will, "Confessions of a Used Program Salesman," a series of seven articles from various issues of *IEEE Software*, reprinted in *Tutorial: Software Reuse: Emerging Technology*, IEEE, 1988.

SECONDARY BIBLIOGRAPHY

1. Books

[Bouldin, 1989] Bouldin, Barbara, *Agents of Change*. Prentice Hall, 1989.

[DeMarco, 1978] DeMarco, Tom, *Structured Analysis and System Specification*. Prentice Hall, 1978.

[Fisher, 1989] Fisher, Alan S., *CASE: Using Software Development Tools*. John Wiley & Sons, 1988.

[Flavin, 1981] Flavin, Matt, *Fundamental Concepts of Information Modeling*. Prentice-Hall, 1990.

[Gane and Sarson, 1979] Gane, Chris and Sarson, Trish, *Structured Systems Analysis: Tools and Techniques*. Prentice Hall, 1979.

[Gardarin and Valduriez, 1989] Gardarin, Georges and Valduriez, Patrick, *Relational Databases and Knowledge Bases*. Addison-Wesley, 1989.

[Humphrey, 1989] Humphrey, Watts, *Managing the Software Process*. Addison-Wesley, 1989.

[McClure, 1989], McClure, Carma, *CASE Is Software Automation*. Prentice Hall, 1989.

[McMenamin and Palmer, 1984] McMenamin, Steve and Palmer, John, *Essential Systems Analysis*. Prentice Hall, 1984.

[Scharbach, 1989] Scharbach, P. N., *Formal Methods: Theory and Practice*. CRC Press, 1989.

2. Articles

[Apple, 1989a] "The Future Belongs to OOP," *Apple Viewpoints*, December 19, 1988.

[Apple, 1989b] "The Power of Object-Oriented Programming," *Apple Direct*, February 1989.

[Banerjee, Chou, Garza, Kim, Woelk, and Ballou, 1987] Banerjee, Jay; Chou, Hong-Tai; Garza, Jorge; Kim, Won; Woelk, Darrell; and Ballou, Nat, "Data Model Issues for Object-Oriented Applications," *ACM Transactions on Office Information Systems*, January 1987.

[Bloom and Zdonik, 1989] Bloom, Tony and Zdonik, Stanley, "Issues in the Design of Object-Oriented Database Programming Languages," *ACM OOPSLA '87 Proceedings*, October 1987.

[Boehm, 1988] Boehm, Barry, "Understanding and Controlling Software Costs," *IEEE Transactions on Software Engineering*, October 1988.

[Booch, 1986] Booch, Grady, "Object-Oriented Development," *IEEE Transactions on Software Engineering*, February 1986.

[Brooks, 1988] Brooks, Fred, "No Silver Bullet," *IEEE Software*, April 1988.

[Bruce, 1988] Bruce, Thomas, "CASE Brought Down to Earth," *Database & Programming Design*, October 1988.

[Cattell and Rogers, 1986] Cattell, R. and Rogers, T., "Combining Object-Oriented and Relational Models of Data," *IEEE International Workshop on Object-Oriented Database Systems Proceedings*, 1986.

[Chen, 1976] Chen, Peter, "The Entity Relationship Model—Toward a Unified View of Data," *ACM Transactions on Database Systems*, March 1976.

[Embley and Woodfield, 1987] Embley, David and Woodfield, Scott, "A Knowledge Structure for Reusing Abstract Data Types," *Proceedings of the Ninth International Conference on Software Engineering*, IEEE, 1987. Also in Tracz, 1988a.

[Fischer, 1989] Fischer, Gerhard, "Human-Computer Interaction in Software: Lessons Learned, Challenges Ahead," *IEEE Software*, January 1989.

[Gerrard, Coleman, and Gallimore, 1990] Gerrard, Christopher; Coleman, Gary; and Gallimore, Robin, "Formal Specification and Design Time Testing," *IEEE Transactions on Software Engineering*, January 1990.

[Ingalls, 1981] Ingalls, David, "Design Principles Behind Smalltalk," *Byte*, August 1981.

[Iscoe, 1988] Iscoe, Neil, "Domain-Specific Reuse: An Object-Oriented and Knowledge-Based Approach," *Tutorial: Software Reuse: Emerging Technology*. IEEE, 1988.

[Jacobsen, 1987] Jacobsen, Ivar, "Object-Oriented Development in an Industrial Environment," *ACM OOPSLA '87 Proceedings*, October 1987.

[Jalote, 1989] Jalote, Pankaj, "Functional Refinement and Nested Objects for Object-Oriented Design," *IEEE Transactions on Software Engineering*, March 1989.

[Katz, Richter, and The, 1987] Katz, Shmuel; Richter, Charles; and The, Khe-Sing, "PARIS: A System for Reusing Partially Interpreted Schemas," *Proceedings of the Ninth International Conference on Software Engineering*. IEEE, 1987. Also in Tracz, 1988a.

[Kim, Ballou, Chou, Garza, and Woelk, 1988] Kim, Won; Ballou, Nat; Chou, Hong-Tai; Garza, Jorge; and Woelk, Darrell, "Integrating an Object-Oriented Programming System with a Database System," *ACM OOPSLA '88 Proceedings,* October 1988.

[Lee, Rissman, D'Ippolito, Plinta, and Scoy, 1988] Lee, Rissman, D'Ippolito, Plinta, and Scoy, "An OOD Paradigm for Flight Simulators," *CMU-SEI Technical Report,* Second Edition, September 1988.

[Lubars, 1987] Lubars, Mitchell, "Wide-Spectrum Support for Software Reusability," *Proceedings from the Workshop on Software Reusability and Maintainability,* National Institute of Software Quality and Productivity, 1987. Also in Tracz, 1988a.

[Martin, 1988] Martin, Jim, "Paper: the Parent of Perfidious Practices," *Defense Science,* July 1988.

[Miller, 1956] Miller, G. A., "The magical number seven, plus or minus two: Some limits on our capacity for processing information," *Psychological Review,* March 1963.

[Miller, 1975] Miller, G. A., "The magic number seven after fifteen years," *Studies in Long Term Memory,* edited by A. Kennedy. Wiley, 1975.

[Millikin, 1989] Millikin, Michael, "Object-Orientation: What It Can Do for You," *Computerworld,* March 13, 1989.

[Parnas, 1972], Parnas, David, "On the Criteria for Decomposing Programs into Modules," *Communications of the ACM,* December 1972.

[Potter and Trueblood, 1988] Potter, William and Trueblood, Robert, "Traditional, Semantic, and Hyper-Semantic Approaches to Data Modeling," *IEEE Computer,* June 1988.

[Ramamoorthy and Sheu, 1988] Ramamoorthy, C. V., and Sheu, Phillip, "Object-Oriented Systems," *IEEE Expert,* Fall 1988.

[Rumbaugh, 1988] Rumbaugh, James, "Controlling Propagation of Operations using Attributes on Relations," *ACM OOPSLA '88 Proceedings,* October 1988.

[Sanden, 1989a] Sanden, Bo, "An Entity-Life Modeling Approach to the Design of Concurrent Software," *Communications of the ACM,* March 1989.

[Sanden, 1989b] Sanden, Bo, "The Case for Eclectic Design of Real-Time Software," *IEEE Transactions on Software Engineering,* March 1989.

[Seidewitz, 1989] Seidewitz, Ed, "Notes on Object-Oriented Analysis and Specification," unpublished notes, December 1988.

[Seidewitz, 1987] Seidewitz, Ed, "Object-Oriented Programming in Smalltalk and Ada," *ACM OOPSLA '87 Proceedings*, October 1987.

[Simos, 1987] Simos, Mark, "The Domain-Oriented Lifecycle: Towards an Extended Process Model for Reusability," *Proceedings from the Workshop on Software Reusability and Maintainability*, National Institute of Software Quality and Productivity, 1987. Also in Tracz, 1988a.

[Smith, 1988] Smith, Connie, "Applying Synthesis Principles to Create Responsive Software Systems," *IEEE Transactions on Software Engineering*, October 1988.

[Smith and Zdonik, 1987] Smith, Karen and Zdonik, Stanley, "Intermedia: A Case Study on the Differences between Relational and Object-Oriented Database Systems," *ACM OOPSLA '87 Proceedings*, September 1987.

[Stroustrop, 1988a] Stroustrup, Bjarne, "A Better C," *Byte*, August 1988.

[Stroustrup, 1988b] Stroustrup, Bjarne, "What is Object-Oriented Programming?", *IEEE Software*, May 1988.

[Tracz, 1987] Tracz, Will, "Reusability Comes of Age," *IEEE Software*, IEEE, July 1987. Also in Tracz, 1988a.

[Tracz, 1988c] Tracz, Will, "RMISE Workshop on Software Reuse Meeting Summary," *Tutorial: Software Reuse: Emerging Technology*, IEEE, 1988. Also in Tracz, 1988a.

[Tracz, 1988d] Tracz, Will, "Software Reuse: Motivators and Inhibitors," *Proceedings of COMPCON*, IEEE, Spring 1987. Also in Tracz, 1988a.

[Tracz, 1988e] Tracz, Will, "Software Reuse Myths," *ACM SIGSOFT Software Engineering Notes*, January 1988. Also in Tracz, 1988a.

[Unland and Schlageter, 1989] Unland, R. and Schlageter, G., "An Object-Oriented Programming Environment for Advanced Database Applications," *Journal of Object-Oriented Programming*, May/June 1989.

[Wing and Nixon, 1989] Wing, J. M. and Nixon, M. R., "Extending Ina Jo™ with Temporal Logic," *IEEE Transactions on Software Engineering*, February 1989. (Ina Jo is a trademark of SDC, now a part of Unisys.)

[Wegner, 1987] Wegner, Peter, "Dimensions of Object-Based Language Design," *ACM OOPSLA '87 Proceedings*, October 1987.

[Zaniolo, Ait-Kaci, Beech, Cammarata, Kerschberg, and Maier, 1986]
Zaniolo, Carlo; Ait-Kaci, Hassan; Beech, David; Cammarata,
Stephanie; Kerschberg, Larry; and Maier, David, "Object-Oriented
Database Systems and Knowledge Systems," *Expert Database
Systems,* edited by Larry Kerschberg, 1986.

3. On-Line Forums

BIX: OOD Conference.
CompuServe: Computer Language Forum.

REFERENCE PUBLICATIONS

[Berryman, 1984] Berryman, Gregg, *Notes on Graphic Design and Visual Communication.* William Kaufmann, 1984.

[Britannica, 1986] *Encyclopaedia Britannica.* Articles on "Behaviour, Animal," "Classification Theory," and "Mood." Encyclopaedia Britannica, Inc., 1986.

[IEEE, 1983] *IEEE Standard Glossary of Software Engineering Terminology* (Standard 729). IEEE, 1983.

[Lanham, 1981] Lanham, Richard A., *Revising Business Prose.* Charles Scribner's Sons, 1981.

[Library of Congress, 1990] *Subjects.* Available in print and on CD-ROM. Library of Congress, 1990.

[Oxford, 1986] *Dictionary of Computing.* Oxford University Press, 1986.

[Rosenau, 1981] Rosenau, Milton, *Successful Project Management.* Wadsworth, 1981.

[Shertzer, 1986] Shertzer, Margaret, *The Elements of Grammar.* Macmillan, 1986.

[Strunk and White, 1979] Strunk Jr., W. and White, E. B., *The Elements of Style.* Macmillan, 1979.

[Webster's, 1977] *Webster's New Twentieth Century Dictionary.* Collins World, 1977.

RELATED PUBLICATIONS

1. Books

[Coad, 1990a] Coad, Peter, *Object-Oriented Analysis*. Seminar notes. Object International (Austin, Texas USA), 1990.

[Coad, 1990b] Coad, Peter, *Object-Oriented Design*. Seminar notes. Object International (Austin, Texas USA), 1990.

[Coad and Yourdon, 1991] Coad, Peter and Yourdon, Edward, *Object-Oriented Design*. Prentice Hall, 1991.

[Yourdon, 1988a] Yourdon, Edward, *Managing the Structured Techniques*. Fourth Edition. Prentice Hall, 1988.

[Yourdon, 1989] Yourdon, Edward, *Modern Structured Analysis*. Prentice Hall, 1989.

2. Articles

[Coad, 1989] Coad, Peter, "OOA: Object-Oriented Analysis," *American Programmer*, Summer 1989.

[Coad and Yourdon, 1990] Coad, Peter and Yourdon, Edward, "OOA—Object-Oriented Analysis," *IEEE Tutorial on System and Software Requirements Engineering*, 1990.

[Yourdon, 1988b] "More on the Future of CASE," *American Programmer*, October 1988.

[Yourdon, 1988c] "Sayonara, Structured Stuff," *American Programmer*, August 1988.

Index

Abstract class, 58
Abstraction,
    data, definition of, 14
    definition, 13–14
    procedural definition of, 13–14
    see also Complexity, principles for managing
Ada, 6, 26, 30–31, 183
American Programmer, 7
Analysis,
    definition of, 18
    difficulties with, 8–12
    methods of,
        data flow, 22–27
        functional decomposition, 20–21
        information modeling, 27–28
        object-oriented, 30–36
Assembly structure, *see Whole-Part structure*
Association,
    definition of, 15
    see also Complexity, principles for managing
Attributes,
    as a criterion for challenging potential objects, 67
    definition of, 119
    how to define,
        checking for special cases,
            with attributes, 128–30
            with instance connections, 131–34
        identifying attributes, 121–25
        identifying instance connections 126–28
            see also Instance connections
        positioning attributes, 125–26
    how to specify, 134–35
    reasons for, 119–20
Bond, Larry, 59
Bouldin, Barbara, 193
Brooks, Fred, 186